Introduction
to Information
Visualization

Introduction to Information Visualization

Transforming Data into Meaningful Information

GERALD BENOÎT

ROWMAN & LITTLEFIELD
Lanham • Boulder • New York • London

Executive Editor: Charles Harmon
Editorial Assistant: Michael Tan
Production Editor: Lara Hahn
Interior Designer: Susan Ramundo
Cover Designer: Sarah Marizan

Credits and acknowledgments of sources for material or information used with permission appear on the appropriate page within the text.

Published by Rowman & Littlefield
An imprint of The Rowman & Littlefield Publishing Group, Inc.
4501 Forbes Boulevard, Suite 200, Lanham, Maryland 20706
www.rowman.com

Unit A, Whitacre Mews, 26-34 Stannary Street, London SE11 4AB

Copyright © 2019 by The Rowman & Littlefield Publishing Group, Inc.

British Library Cataloguing in Publication Information Available

Library of Congress Cataloging-in-Publication Data

Names: Benoît, Gerald, author.
Title: Introduction to information visualization : transforming data into meaningful information / Gerald Benoît.
Description: Lanham : Rowman & Littlefield, 2019. | Includes bibliographical references and index.
Identifiers: LCCN 2018038992 (print) | LCCN 2018044869 (ebook) | ISBN 9781538125090 (electronic) | ISBN 9781538118344 (cloth : alk. paper) | ISBN 9781538118351 (pbk. : alk. paper)
Subjects: LCSH: Information visualization.
Classification: LCC QA76.9.I52 (ebook) | LCC QA76.9.I52 B46 2019 (print) | DDC 001.4/226—dc23
LC record available at https://lccn.loc.gov/2018038992

∞™ The paper used in this publication meets the minimum requirements of American National Standard for Information Sciences—Permanence of Paper for Printed Library Materials, ANSI/NISO Z39.48-1992.

Printed in the United States of America

To David Crabill and Ryan Vanderweit,
who encouraged during difficult times.

CONTENTS

An online supplement is available at
https://bix.digital/infovis/index.html.

PREFACE

Why this monograph? There are plenty of visually intriguing texts out there. Many are steeped in computer science, demonstrating step-by-step methods for mapping data to graphics. Others are mainly artistic, delving into the visual aspects of design, but with little exposure to data and text processing. Collectively, these books offer valuable perspectives across many aspects of the field. But no text truly presents an explanation of the data + aesthetics aspects of information visualization (InfoVis). We need a book that crosses disciplines, helping people to *reflect on their decisions* and to develop skills in both arts *and* data. I aim through this book to accomplish this by practicing information visualization from the ground up.

Contemporary librarianship, information science, digital humanities, Open Government movements, computer science, and many more disciplines require new professionals to demonstrate considerable technical competence. Upon entering their various fields, graduate students have successfully applied their skills to create new systems and services. The purpose of this monograph is to help both the neophyte and the experienced professional master the visual and technological skills necessary to participate fully in the rapidly expanding realm of visualization.

The scope of this text includes a review of HTML and CSS before introducing a powerful JavaScript library called d3.js (https://d3js.org/). By creating interactive information visualization websites, the student is introduced to the most important skills and issues related to data sources and data types, preparation of data, client-server architecture, understanding the role of aesthetics in message construction, and the larger field of aesthetics and ethics in information, and will gain a background in commercial products. The focus of work in this book is to create a "proof of concept" demonstrating one's understanding of the technology, the end user, and principles of design. It is intended for "information professionals" who want to bridge the user, technical, and data services, and increase services for their patrons.

Unlike other books, this guide offers software for a complete library service, helping end users—students, staff, administration, faculty and researchers, and the general public—select and design an appropriate visualization *as well as* providing the tools that will convert their data for the visualization. The result is to enable the user to focus on presenting, explaining, and exploring their data.

Moreover, the integration of aesthetics and information services is a unique addition to the literature, allowing information professionals to "own the message." We can integrate the principles of information service and technology that contribute to the patrons' transition from "data" to "meaningful information."

We offer real examples. Some are based on real students' actual work. Others are based on teaching technical skills about data and scripting that address institutional interests. Ultimately, the complete information system for visualization provided in the appendixes is an actual test service at Harvard University Libraries.

Choosing what to include and what to exclude in a course is exceedingly challenging. I strive to present an accurate representation of the entire field, gladly recognizing others' accomplishments and contributions. This monograph is based on updates to materials to teach the product of the past several years, evolving as I taught undergraduate computer science courses, mixed graduate/undergraduate classes on health informatics, computer science, business, and library and information science (LIS). This book reflects my experience as a computer and information science professor, as an active systems analyst/programming consultant, and as a former art director for an international advertising firm.

Students enrolled in the InfoVis course for a wide spectrum of reasons. Sometimes the course is required for their major. Sometimes they wish to build upon their background in technology or in the arts. Students working in libraries, archives, museums, computer science, and business have completed the course. With this range of experience and expectations, the incoming students' skill sets range from the eager neophyte to the greatly experienced in some fields, but limited exposure in the broader topic. The course is designed with a few expectations about the readers' background: basic knowledge of SFTP, HTML5, CSS, and JavaScript. Students should have access to a web server or feel comfortable running their own server on their computers. I recommend the pre-installed Apache web server on the Mac, or downloading and installing a server for Unix and Windows.

Unlike other texts, which include slides and additional readings, this monograph is supplemented by a website. The site hosts updates to the literature, practice activities, and sample visualizations. Readers are welcome to offer suggestions, point out errors, and communicate with others interested in the topic of visualization.

Students completing this course leave with greater confidence in their technical skills. Their skills are proven and easily marketable to future employers. The emphasis in this book on students' reflections about their design, data, and interactivity choices will aid in understanding the value of the user experience, information-seeking behavior, server technology, and real leadership in providing important services to their communities.

In the end, what will you, the student, gain? I know that students gain new ideas and perspectives about ethics and graphics in information. Equally, they develop fluency in hands-on technical skills (applying d3 and comparing this experience with commercial products), running scripts to convert their data, and building an interactive visualization site in which they can take pride. For students who wish to apply their knowledge to popular commercial products, particularly Tableau (https://www.tableau.com/), they'll approach commercial visualization tools with a more informed, critical eye on the role and presentation of data. Most of all, information professionals will "own" their understanding of data and visualization, allowing them to better serve their patrons or customers. They are able to *participate* in the cutting edge of research, service, and information systems. They appreciate the *beauty of information.*

ONLINE COMPANION SITE

There's an online companion site for this course that hosts living examples, updates, and errata. You're invited to participate on the site, too, sharing your questions, solutions, and ideas. For most readings, there is a partner design lab. At the conclusion of the course, there is a complete interactive information visualization service documentation for libraries. The scripts, interfaces, examples, and other documents are based on a Harvard University Libraries' project to integrate and support InfoVis in the repertoire of students, administrators, and researchers. Comments are welcomed via benoit@fas.harvard.edu, gb@bix.digital, or on the companion site, https://bix.digital/infovis/index.html. The site hosts links, demos, source code, project documentation, design labs, and an online course website.

On the companion website, you will find chapter 8, "Deploying an InfoVis Service (the Harvard Libraries project documentation)," and the following appendixes:

- Data and Information Ecosystems
- More about Data, Learning, and Visualization

ACKNOWLEDGMENTS

Thanks to the anonymous reviewers. Thanks, too, to the students and professionals who studied in the InfoVis course that is the basis of this text: Anastasia Weigle, University of Maine; Ceilyn Boyd and Hugh Truslow, Harvard University; Bonnie Gardner, Shayne Murray, and Jessica Hoffman, the students in the systems analysis course who completed the design for the Harvard Libraries Visualization Project; and the publisher.

## CHAPTER 1

Introduction

Why Information Visualization? Why Skills + Data + Communication?

In this chapter we will start two streams of thought: one about aesthetic and message construction features, and one to introduce the computer technologies used in visualization practices.

An introduction to information visualization (InfoVis) is a valuable preliminary to many aesthetic, communicative, technical, and social aspects of data. These first steps are not without a little controversy.

InfoVis is an especially human behavior. At one time, the visualization of data was but an alternative way of presenting numbers to an expert in some field. In 1940, *American Demographics*, a leading journal for statisticians, described the use of images to represent data instead of using the traditional printed tables—to the shock of the readership. The use of images to represent statistics was not universally nor happily accepted. We see the beautiful outcome, however, in statistician Edmund Tufte's series of monographs recounting the history and approaches to applying visualization to help people comprehend the majesty of numbers.

Until the late 1970s, and perhaps continuing today, the idea of people using graphic languages to express numbers and relationships within and among the data was a highly empiricist activity. The sense was that humans, as an unknowable "black box," accept visual stimuli inputs and behave in a certain way as the resulting output. Measuring the before-and-after difference could determine the effectiveness of the visualization. Today, researchers and practitioners of InfoVis still give due regard to the benefits of this kind of investigation, the role played by the biology of sight, and the impact that color, composition, and typography exert on interpretation.

Contemporary information visualization work is entering new terrain, uncharted, yet with many signposts. For example, engineers, computer scientists, and data mining experts have embraced some of the knowledge of graphic designers' practices. Designers necessarily have greater facility with the computer, data models, scripting, and programming. Collectively, the trend is to view information visualization practice as an almost community-driven event. Articles like Brent Dykes's "Data Storytelling: The Essential Data Science Skill Everyone Needs" (2016) make it clear that visualization is part of the public and business scene.

There is the increasing digitization and quantification of society. In our jobs and in our social lives, the idea of "argument by numbers" dominates. For instance, a reference librarian's success is not measured or valued by the impact the librarian has on the patron, but rather the number of patrons served during a work shift. Recording and displaying numbers without context and comment means that it is easy to lie by accident or by design with statistics, or to present an entirely different message than intended. This happens when the application of InfoVis is not *understood*, or there is a disconnect between what the audience sees in the data and what the creator of the graphic intended in his or her choices in layout, color scheme, and data types. When these data + visual facets don't cohere, the viewer cannot rightfully interpret the visual language and understand the intended message.

Meanwhile, the pervasiveness of computers and the vastly simplified tools to create interactive visualizations enable almost anyone to create graphics and websites. Today online training sites such as W3Schools provide useful education in the fundamentals of today's digital world. There students can learn HTML, CSS (cascading style sheet), PHP, Python, MySQL, JavaScript, and more. Products for development and visualization frequently are created and offered gratis on sites such as GitHub or developers' home pages. Such tools invigorate non–computer scientists to express themselves on the Internet, as indeed they ought to.

The result of these trends is to stimulate interest in all things visual, changing people's expectations of data delivered by computer devices, be they laptops, apps, phones, or desktop computers. Furthermore, there is an increasing need for recent graduates and established professionals to create and to use "information visualizations" on the job.

JUST WHAT IS INFORMATION VISUALIZATION?

Let's start with what it is not. Many websites host "information visualizations" that are static images, and so (for us) are "information graphics," data-filled picture using icons, charts, and text that must be as much experienced as "read" to gain the knowledge intended by the design. Viewing an information graphic can be an aesthetically pleasing activity. Interpreting the data, on the other hand, requires engaging with the image, breaking apart and viewing the composition, the data, and other visual messages on the page.

But an "information graphic" is the same as a painting: In the ancient Greek text *Phædrus*, Socrates asks Phædrus, his student, "What happens when you ask a picture a question? It goes on saying the same thing," meaning the visualization offers what it can. But we need more to understand the message. The examples in figure 1.1 are similar to information visualizations, but have static designs. One is the typically expected graphic language of data. The other uses data to form an unanticipated visage. But if we add some interactivity, data sources, and then address the "three Vs" (variability, volume, variety of data), we can transform them into interactive visualizations.

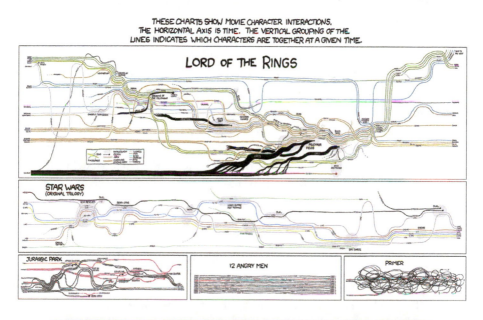

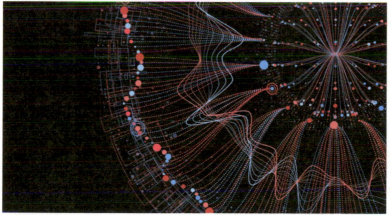

FIGURE 1.1 Visualizing data into a compelling story doesn't have to be highly technical—it can be fun and aesthetic, provided the data is interpretable. *http://forum.darkside.com.br/vb/showthread.php?t=45907*

We need to be able to read the language of visualizations as well as apply the tools of creating useful visualizations. "Information visualization" is the purposively designed graphic representation of data so that a viewer can gain facts, expose the unexpected in the data, and engage with the visualization, such that the viewer really understands the data, very much as if she or he were conversing with the data. It is only as the result of this internal conversation or external discussion with colleagues that this otherwise static display of data helps people use the data in a meaningful, informed way. This is the transformation from data to meaningful information. Stated more succinctly: *A well-designed "information visualization" is interactive, allowing viewers to converse with the data: gaining knowledge, exposing insights, and engaging with the data in unexpected ways. It is only through these conversations that the otherwise static display of data transforms into meaningful information.*

The graphic must be approachable, balancing the amount of data, size of the output device (monitor), and the user experience. In this image from a research project titled "Do Breast Cancer Cell Lines Provide a Relevant Model of the Patient Tumor Methylome?" (figure 1.2), the volume and visual expression of the data are better suited for a statistically informed, biomedical audience. Recognizing the impact the audience has on the success of the visualization is a vital point when designing the graphic.

When faced with data, we must ask: "Why would a visualization be useful?"

- To be part of explaining a problem
- To decide what to do, informed by the statistical underpinnings of the data
- To answer a question more deeply
- To reduce the amount of displayed data into manageable chunks, but allowing details on demand

Advising a computer science student on which path to take is a good example of breaking down a question and taking the first steps toward visualizing the answer (figure 1.3).

To discern trends in visualizations, consider a continuum of degrees of dynamism or interaction, and the amount of computational power needed to create or use the graphic. If considering visualization from a *data-centric* perspective, there is a continuum progressing from the world of graphic arts per se toward graphics aimed at expressing data (figure 1.4), then toward graphics that allow the user to explore data and finally express large volumes of data in a digital environment. These large collections of data may be purposively designed for sustained engagement, or mined.

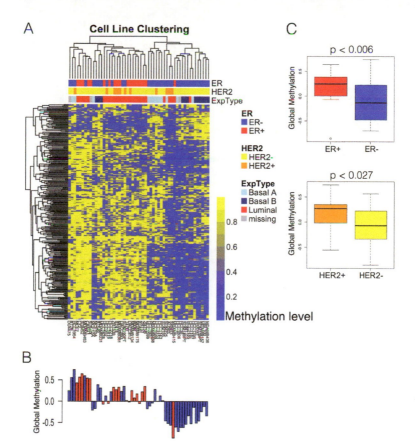

FIGURE 1.2 An example of an extremely complex data set, in which the visual representation is a challenge to interpret. (Data represents the patient tumor methylome). *http://journals.plos.org/plosone/article?id=10.1371/journal.pone.0105545*

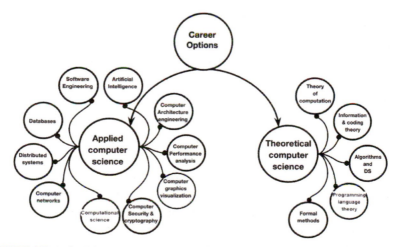

FIGURE 1.3 A decision-tree graphic that helps decision making. It demonstrates the way data can be cast as a whole ("career options"), and then divides the problem into increasingly smaller sets. *https://medium.com/readers-writers -digest/beginners-guide-to-computer-science-engineering-361ae1682f5c*

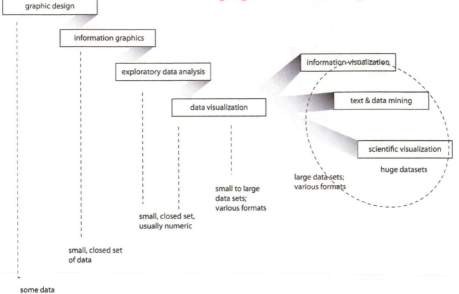

A merging of worlds: design and data

FIGURE 1.4 One model of the continuum of relationships in the graphic/visual information world. *Courtesy of the author*

Many streams of work and research have emerged recently, given the emphasis on data or computing. One is visual analytics. Others are subsumed in the "big data" movement, in which "information ecologies" focus on techniques to reduce the astonishingly large sets of live data to computationally useful sizes and include statistical analysis, using tools such as Snowflake, MapReduce, Apache Hadoop, and Spark.

The popular statistical program R (https://www.r-project.org) by itself requires a knowledge of statistics, and will generate visual representations of the data. If these data are static, they're just "information graphics." R has a graphic user interface plug-in you can use, too (http://www.sciviews.org/_rgui/) and several other associated statistical and graphic projects (https://www.r-project.org/other-projects.html).

Regardless of the casual use of the terms *information graphics* and *information visualizations*, the main points are the same:

- The computer software to create images are increasingly the same for their display (e.g., Adobe Illustrator (SVG), Oracle, and many others).
- The raw sources of the data, likewise, are either in spreadsheets, or some relational database management system (RDBMS) tables, or in .xml or .json, among other formats.

- Despite the name, exploratory data analysis (EDA) is the set of basic bar charts, pie charts, and such. These are usually part of any spreadsheet program, and many .js libraries, such as Raphael.js; it's debatable whether Tableau, Python's charting libraries, and others are EDA or more.
- Interactive data visualization, such as d3.js, Tableau, SAS, SPSS, IBM—web or stand-alone.
- Stand-alone applications, usually combining statistical analysis with (interactive) displays and options to see the statistical evidence for an assertion . . . but be aware of "lift" (e.g., Watson).
- Or a visualization architecture ("information environment") such as Apache Hadoop.

Increasingly, we will find online tools where the end user (you) can upload a data file and the website will create a visualization or download a library and use JavaScript to assist with making graphics. Take a look at the various projects on Vega (https://vega.github.io/vega/ and https://vega.github.io):

Vega 3.0	Vega-Lite	Lyra
Polestar	Voyager	Compass

Google, naturally, has gotten into the visualization game with its Google Charts (https://developers.google.com/chart/).

The Vega project also includes plug-ins, extension code packages that facilitate creating data generated in other programs. For example, to expand R's capabilities, there's the ggvis package; others include Vega.jl (for Julia programming language), the MediaWiki Graph extension, and Cedar, to integrate with ArcGIS (a popular geographic information system program, https://www.arcgis.com/features/index.html). Python, too, supports a surprising number of semi-interactive visualizations. In short, we can classify visualization tools into three groups:

1. Stand-alone visualization applications
2. Tools for creating interactive visualizations (usually web-based)
3. Tools that visualize statistical data, either as a built-in part of the program or as a plug-in

STAND-ALONE VISUALIZATION APPLICATIONS

- Tableau: https://www.tableau.com
- IBM Visualization Designer: https://www-01.ibm.com/common/ssi/cgi-bin/ssialias?htmlfid=YTD03025GBEN&appname=wwwsearch
- SPSS: http://www.spss.com.hk/software/statistics/vizdesigner/
- SAS: https://www.sas.com/en_us/software/visual-analytics.html

Depending on your background and needs, you might want to download and experiment with demo versions.

TOOLS FOR CREATING VISUALIZATIONS

There are many tools for creating designs for visualizations and for building the actual computer-based product. It is useful to note that Adobe Illustrator or Gimp facilitate creating both printed graphics as well as the SVG (scalable vector graphics) data needed for many visualizations. Because both graphic designers and information visualization specialists start their designs using the same tools, there are naturally commonalities inviting the technical student to study graphics and the design student to study data.

The most powerful and most approachable do-it-yourself visualization is Mike Bostock's d3.js library (https://d3js.org; see figure 1.5). This site hosts many tutorials, examples of work by others, and is a source of inspiration. To use this library,

FIGURE 1.5 Homepage of the D3 JavaScript Library. *https://d3js.org*

you should be comfortable with HTML, CSS, and fundamentals of JavaScript, because integrating the d3 library allows you to create interactive visualizations.

It isn't necessary at the outset to possess great design skills (see figure 1.6). This example demonstrates a designer's toolkit of designs based on his understanding of mathematics and data.

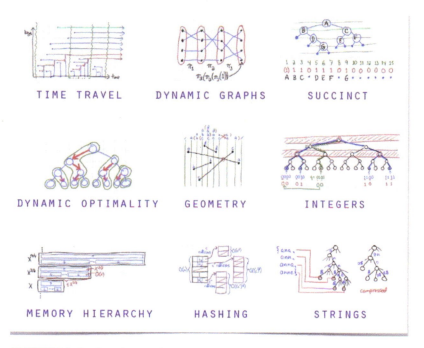

FIGURE 1.6 Design the graphic before creating it. Sketching helps in understanding the type of story to be told by balancing the data types with the visualization. *https://www.pinterest.com/explore/data-structures/*

Knowing what graphic representation to apply is partially a function of the data themselves and partially from the designer's understanding of the target audience viewing the graphic. The Internet and publications have many recommended charting types. I believe the InfoVis specialist must understand the data, interactivity, graphic design, aesthetics, the display device (such as a computer monitor), and the audience in order to create the "best," most truthful, most interpretable visualization. Table 1.1 is an example of one designer's analysis of what type of chart to create given the purpose of the visualization based on the data.

Of course, this should not suggest that our designs are not aesthetically pleasing. For example, Fastcodedesign's representation is an intriguing way to explain prime numbers (figure 1.7).

TABLE 1.1	
Purpose of visualization	**Recommended chart type**
Compare data side by side	Bar chart
Combine absolute and relative values	Combo chart
Make selections to reduce dataset	Filter pane
Indicate ratio	Gauge
Display a performance value	KPI
Display trends over time	Line chart
Display point and area data	Map
Display ratio to total	Pie chart
Create a cross table view of data and to summarize data	Pivot table
Display correlation of measures	Scatter plot
Display numbers and values	Table
Display text, images, links, and measures	Text and image
Display hierarchical data	Treemap
Compare range and distribution for groups of numerical data	Box plot
	Distribution plot
Display distribution of numerical data over a continuous interval, or a certain time period	Histogram

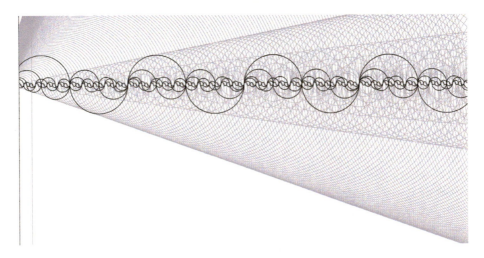

FIGURE 1.7 Here the beauty of data representing prime numbers, exposing the art of mathematics and the mathematics of art. *https://www.fastcodedesign.com /1670397/infographic-visualizing-prime-numbers-for-people-who-suck-at-math*

These are all great projects, and may suggest to you the range of interest in creating visualizations where both the interactivity and the data are shareable. But notice, too, that these options require considerable programming and statistical experience. Such projects underscore that the *data*—and that's important—as well as the creators' understanding of aesthetics, message construction, and message receipt by the viewers of the graphics and visualizations, are what give meaning and value.

Over the course of this book, you will find fully explained demonstration code samples, a term-length course website with additional "design labs," readings and resources, and more, available at the companion site, https://bix.digital/infovis/. These are designed to work together to help you explore and enjoy the *beautiful in information*.

REFERENCES

Dykes, B. (2016, March 16). Data storytelling: The essential data science skill everyone needs. *Forbes*. Retrieved Mar 22, 2018 from https://www.forbes.com/sites/brentdykes /2016/03/31/data-storytelling-the-essential-data-science-skill-everyone-needs/#2c6a 880652ad

Plato. (1995). *Phaedrus*. (Woodruff, Trans.) Indianapolis, IN: Hackett.

## CHAPTER 2

The Ethics/Aesthetics of Information

In this reading, we turn to notions and variability of "aesthetics," the role of intentionality in message construction, and will contextualize the whole as a stressful engagement between the locus of interpretations in any visual—be it "art" or an "information visualization." The expressions in this reading may not be my opinions—they are challenging ideas drawn from the literature to engage students, particularly those with an educational background in philosophy, literary studies, or art criticism.

There are independent sections (defining information, InfoVis, and aesthetics) that collectively will be applied to why we use computers to generate visuals; how those visuals, like any other information resource, are both helpful and reflect the intentions of the creator; and the complex relationships we balance so as not to deceive viewers of our interactive information visualizations.

Discussing information visualization (InfoVis) leads us to fundamentals. What is information? What role does visualization contribute to "being informed"? What are the activities converting data into information?

A first course in information visualization is a great introduction to many aesthetic, communicative, technical, and social aspects of data. Like any art form, InfoVis is an especially human behavior. At one time, the visualization of data was but an alternative way of presenting numbers to an expert in some field. In 1940, a statistical journal, *American Demographics*, described the use of images instead of long tables—to the shock of the readership. Until the late 1970s, and perhaps continuing today, the idea of people using graphic languages to express numbers and relationships within and between the data was a highly empiricist activity. The sense was that humans, as an unknowable "black box," accept visual stimuli as inputs and behave in a certain way as the output, which could be measured to determine the effectiveness of the visualization. Today researchers and practitioners of InfoVis still hold in regard the benefits of this kind of investigation, the role played by the biology of sight, and the impact that color exerts in interpretation. But there's more: contemporary information visualization work is entering a new terrain, uncharted, yet with many signposts. Engineers, computer scientists, and data mining experts have embraced some of the knowledge of graphic designers' practices. Designers necessarily have greater facility with the computer, data models, and scripting and programming. Collectively, the trend is to view information visualization practice as an almost community-driven event (figure 2.1). Many authors note how visualization is storytelling; suggesting that InfoVis work is a collaboration of problem solving, workflows, presentation of candidate visual solutions, and shared critique.

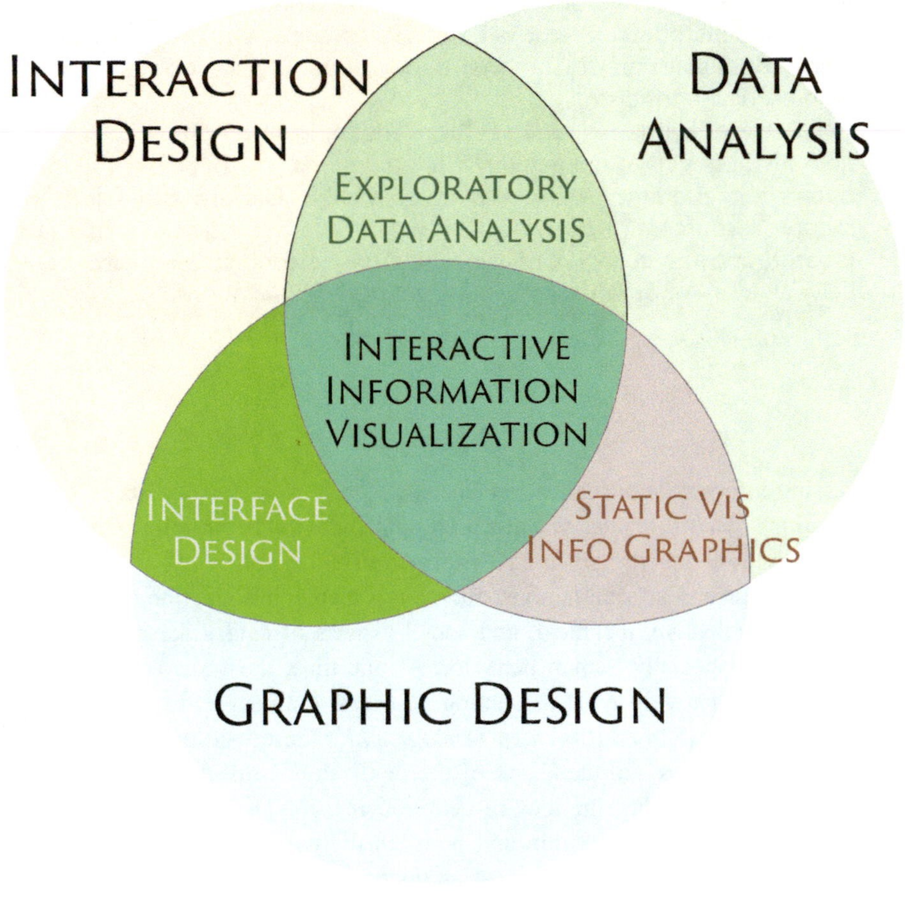

INTERACTION DESIGN

DATA ANALYSIS

EXPLORATORY DATA ANALYSIS

INTERACTIVE INFORMATION VISUALIZATION

INTERFACE DESIGN

STATIC VIS INFO GRAPHICS

GRAPHIC DESIGN

FIGURE 2.1 Venn diagram of main work function areas in InfoVis. *Courtesy of the author*

The great changes come from several sources. There is the increasing digitization and quantification of society. In our jobs and increasingly in our social lives, the idea of "argument by numbers" dominates. For instance, the public service activities of the reference librarian aren't measured and valued by the impact the librarian has on a patron, but rather by the number of patrons served during a work shift. But it is easy to lie with statistics, or to present an entirely different message than one intends. This happens when the application of InfoVis is not understood, or there is a disconnect between the audience seeing the data and the creator of the graphic. The layout, color scheme, and data types don't cohere in a way the viewer can successfully interpret the visual language and understand the intended message.

Certainly the pervasiveness of computers and the vastly simplified tools to create interactive visualizations enable almost anyone to create graphics and websites. Today online training sites such as w3schools provide really useful education in the fundamentals of today's digital world. There you can learn HTML, CSS, PHP, MySQL, XML, JavaScript and more. Products for development and visualization frequently are created and offered gratis on sites such as GitHub or the developers' homepages.

The result of these trends is to stimulate interest in all things visual, changing people's expectations of data delivered by computer devices, be they laptops, apps, phones, or desktop computers. Furthermore, people expect to create and to use information visualizations on the job. That is why we are here. We wish to establish a solid foothold in this new land, even though others hold different positions, so that we, too, can participate with confidence and skill in informed ways in the visual language of data that is the future.

Just what is information visualization? Let's start with what it is not. Many books and websites host "information visualizations" that are static images: a data-filled picture using icons, charts, and text that must be read to gain the knowledge intended by the design. There is no end user interactivity. Viewing an information graphic can be an aesthetically pleasing activity. Interpreting the data, on the other hand, requires engaging with the image, breaking apart and viewing the composition, the data, the other visual messages on the page. But an "information graphic" is the same as a painting. Socrates asked, "What happens when you ask a picture a question? It goes on saying the same thing," meaning the visualization offers what it can . . . but we need more to understand the message.

This suggests that we need to be able to read the language of visualizations as well as apply the tools of creating useful visualizations. InfoVis is the purposively designed graphic representation of data such that the viewer can gain facts, expose the unexpected in the data, and engage with the visualization. It is through interaction with the data via the graphics and computer that the viewer really understands the data, very much as if she or he had a conversation. It's only the result of this internal conversation or external discussion with colleagues that the otherwise static display of data helps people apply the data in a meaningful, informed way—hence, information. For example, to know a list of capital cities is to know data; to learn about one of those cities as you decide where to visit and make your decision, you've progressed from "using data" to "creating information."

To discern trends in visualizations, let's consider a continuum of degrees of dynamism or interaction and the amount of computational power needed to create or use the graphic (figure 2.2).

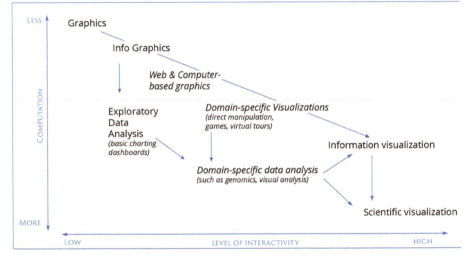

A MODEL OF VISUALIZATION EFFORTS BY DEGREES OF COMPUTER-POWER AND USER-INTERACTIVITY

FIGURE 2.2 Another model of the relationships of data + visual languages. "Static" refers to the degree of end user interactivity. Graphics allow no interaction; visualizations rely upon it. *Courtesy of the author*

PHILOSOPHICAL, COMMUNICATIVE, AND ETHICAL COMPONENTS

There's the usual introductory model of data → information → knowledge . . . but this is insufficient for us (figure 2.3). The world of information visualization has already impacted this traditional model by integrating not only the notion of "wisdom," but the tried-and-true applications of knowledge with great reliability of results, decision making, and confidence (figure 2.4). What's more, the visual representation of this trend is evinced by InfoVis practices: drawing an idea, and then expressing it through computer technology.

KNOWLEDGE

Insight, experience, understanding

INFORMATION

data in context; classified, calculated (for numbers), organized

DATA

facts & figures; "semantic-level" data; not organized

The usual "data-info-knowledge" triangle

FIGURE 2.3 The traditional data-info-knowledge pyramid. *Courtesy of the author*

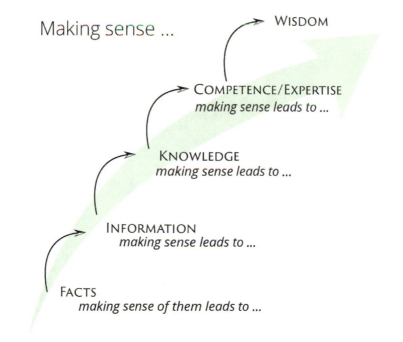

Making sense ...   WISDOM

COMPETENCE/EXPERTISE
making sense leads to ...

KNOWLEDGE
making sense leads to ...

INFORMATION
making sense leads to ...

FACTS
making sense of them leads to ...

FIGURE 2.4 Integrating skills, sense-making, and wisdom. *Courtesy of the author*

When considering these figures, we begin to see some of the most important ways of thinking about visualizations: data, some contextualization in the extraction and identification of data, links between these concepts . . . and then significantly, indeed vitally, some pattern or something that defies a pattern. In data mining, this is called an "interesting event." The physical/graphic representation of that identified curiosity is a major activity in InfoVis. The testing and refining of that new knowledge derived from the visualization is what leads ultimately to wisdom. Some of the cognitive activities of the creators (you) and the viewers (your patrons) are expressed as "clustering," "association," "relating," and "classifying" . . . and in the end require interpretation that synthesizes the interesting events and then submits them to appropriate tests. These tests may be any number of qualitative (such as human-computer interaction studies) or quantitative (empirical) studies—very commonly statistics.

Randomly assigning dots (figure 2.5) that are representations of underlying facts (data), then the iterative process of questioning relationships, leads to an understanding of how and why data points *may* be associated. Reflecting on the need for the data revises what data should be associated together, which are associated closely but not enough and may constitute their own group . . . until finally we arrive at reliable, validated, comprehensible "information" that we apply skillfully in our context of application.

Data	Questioning	Becoming Informed	Knowledge/Skills

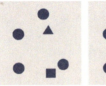

These are associated because ... *Class this one differently because...* *Maybe cluster?*

Synthesizing these sets suggests a more powerful association between the two lower ones ... and a useful different classification for another

Validate *Synthesize*

Expertise in the data + context = interpretation

expressed as a random display of dots

In what ways might these data's relationships, position, color suggest to a reason for their associations and a **recognized potential** *for their use*

The result of cognitive/communicative engagement leads viewer to understand the data, their relationships, the potential utility as well as how s/he might explain to others their applicability. Interpretation of the potentiality of the data through the medium of visual language

Stability in data sets, interpretation, and applicability (or a coherence) that is reliably applied with consistent outcomes. Interpretation of the context of application.

FIGURE 2.5 A visual suggestion of sense-making from data, adding actions (clustering, associating, relating, and classifying) to create "information" and taking the results of interpretation (validating the data and synthesizing the results into one's information needs) as "knowledge." (Expanded from http://www .nickdiakopoulos.com/2011/12/16/data-information-knowledge-visualization/, which includes only data, information, and knowledge.) *Courtesy of the author*

What are data? Data, to my thinking, are the result of human work, of facts, of naming, or of identifying tangible and intangible things. It's a pretty powerful idea that we can assign an identity to something and then use the representation of the identity to communicate the idea to others. For example, to create a lamp and create the word *lamp* is to identify something in the world and to be able to share that concept with someone else, without relying on the physical act of pointing to the lamp. The power of naming is so great that the Book of Genesis is the first creative activities of Adam and Eve. If we created a town and name it, we can use that name to introduce awareness of this site to *others*—hence, "communication."

By "communicating" a name to someone else, we encounter some important points. One is the idea of a *message*. What is a message? Let's distinguish some aspects of a message. One is the idea that you want to share. Another is the way you represent that idea. Usually we have a thought and then express a representation of that thought through words (an oral utterance) or by text (a written proposition). As an alternative or a supplement, we rely on images—a postcard, pictures from your digital phone, a sketch on a napkin—both to convey our idea and to increase the certainty that we are indeed sharing our idea with someone else.

In some research and practice fields, we might say that the expression of our idea has intentionality (a purposeful context, linguistic register) that needs to be interpreted by the recipient, and applied in the real world. Breaking down the utterance, we identify both roles and vital facets. The roles: someone has chosen to share something (the speaker; in visual terms, this is the artist). Someone listening to the message probably asked a question and this utterance is the response. How well does the answer suit the question?

This is the key. Can the person seeing or hearing a message understand or gain some useful impression of the message at first glance? For instance, if I greet you with a cheery "Bonjour!" you may not understand it but the context of the utterance suggests a greeting. If I greeted a known friend with a frown and muttered "bonjour," the greeting is the same but clearly the feeling of the message, or the affective aspect—a contributor to the interpretive possibilities of a message—is negative. The interpretation of the person hearing/seeing the message is not a positive welcome but a sarcastic or warning message. We must recognize that the creator of a message, be it oral, textual, or visual, intends to convey some meaning to a recipient, and that recipient may understand the intended message or may not. The tools people use to interpret a message as correctly as they can start with their mind and their understanding of shared symbols, expectations, and norms. An old friend with experiences will contextualize my grunted greeting in one way, perhaps recognizing I'm having a bad week. A stranger has no such private knowledge, and the result will be a miscommunication. Creating an intended message in the context of sharing with others in the same cultural/visual environment helps the recipient interpret the message as we intend. Hence the rise in courses and studies in "visual intelligence."

Another main part is *communication*. If we have nothing to say, there is no message. If we choose to start a conversation with someone, then there is implied a sense of relationship between the "speaker/hearer" or "artist/viewer" pair. Greeting a stranger on the bus with "Hello" does not imply anything more than a socially normative behavior: it is appropriate to greet strangers in this common setting, the bus. Greeting a friend on that same bus with a peck on the cheek may be acceptable as a social norm, but that same peck on a stranger is an assault.

We have, then, a message, an expression of that message, the social normative setting that allows presenting that message, and we have the issues that affect surface-level interpretation of the message and then the deeper meaning-construction of the message.

SEEING, AESTHETICS, AND DATA

Students approaching visualization for the first time bring much knowledge of their other fields of study. Many communications, humanities, literature, and philosophy students have encountered some of the ideas that follow in their undergraduate work. So let's start here and slowly walk across some main themes to suggest how those backgrounds apply fruitfully in InfoVis. Later we'll focus more on the data, design, and technology of visualizations.

It hasn't been popular for a while in many academic and industry circles to consider the role of *interpretation*. Indeed, the trend is to diminish the cognitive, personal, and social roles of people to be fed passively a message and its interpretation. Some human-computer interaction texts, such as *Don't Make Me Think* (Krug, 2014), clearly show that some want the end user not to engage cognitively but rather follow the trend of data—be they images, text, and media—to adopt without critique the sender's message. This implies that the message, when adopted by the end user, functions as truthful, as appropriate for the end user's interests and needs, as not needing investigation or communication. While in the abstract this approach may not seem difficult, it is fraught with intellectual, ethical, social, and now informational, challenges.

There is an astonishingly long history in the West, as far as I know, about "interpretation of messages." How do people read or hear or see someone else's message such that the creator's intended message is the one that the hearer/viewer receives?

As early as the ancient Greek philosophers, the idea of "interpretation" was a hotly debated, vigorously investigated question. By the mid-eighteenth century, a German theologian, Friedrich Schleiermacher (1768–1834), embarked on a systematic exploration of what it means to interpret something. As a Lutheran pastor, he focused on the Bible and attempted to understand the Enlightenment and Protestant Christianity. He reflected on the body and soul, wondered about the relationship between the ego's "true identity" and relationship to "higher life." In the end, Schleiermacher's efforts impacted quite greatly the field of hermeneutics. (This is noteworthy in information studies because hermeneutics are a popular research technique.) Schleiermacher cast the Bible and other engagements as "texts" and understood that "reading a text" was not a systematic or language-based approach, but an "art of understanding." There was a "discourse" between the text and the person engaging with, or interpreting, the text. Certainly we cannot review here the complexities of the topic of interpretation, nor of Schleiermacher's notion (and the notions of Plato, Heidegger, Derrida, Gadamer and Ricœur, Kant and Fichte, among others) of how we know what we think we know from reading, speaking, and engaging in the world. However, we can get a feeling for the great concern people have had over generations for interpreting a message and the need for certainty in accepting a message's content. There is necessarily a bond or some form of relationship between the creator of the message, the recipient of the message, and the society that both share.

In the world of computer science, information science, data science, data mining, and big data, the philosophical questions of interpretation and of its relationship to "truthfulness" are not often considered. There is one body of researchers to whom the questions of truthfulness and applicability are set aside because data and algorithms extract and present data whose purpose is to be (somehow) automatically useful and automatically validated through empirical (here, read mathematical) techniques. However, others do believe that the issue of interpretation at the nexus of computing and visual languages is the future. There are trends in computer science and in information science, and in the visual arts, to recognize the social application of these fields and how the work of professionals in these fields impacts society. For instance, Knight noted that "biased algorithms are everywhere, but no one seems to care" (2017). Perhaps a bit harsh, but Knight's work does clue us in that the issue of ethics and computing are active areas of investigation.

DESIGN

Consider now graphic design. Many of us use templates when creating PowerPoint slides or even web pages, and the results may be graphically appealing. Aesthetic presentation is important because the aspects of a design are powerful enticements to engage the viewer. The composition, color, typography, and overall design impact the viewer's sense/affective view of the image and color the interpretation of the message. Commercial templates often apply trendy color schemes and culturally identifiable feelings—the way a haphazard font style is used for children's websites, sans serif fonts may look more formal and so are used in business presentations, and Victorian-era fonts are used to suggest the grandeur of the BBC television shows "Downton Abbey" or "Victoria," or campy horror movies of the 1930s through the 1950s.

Some texts identify dominant composition or layout styles. Castro, in *Slide:ology* (2008) presents a great, reduced version of popular Western layouts. There are also websites and guidebooks that suggest color pairing pallets, type combinations, and interactive sites (such as paletton.com) to help you identify color combinations that convey the feeling of your intended message as well as providing the computer codes to represent the color.

For an information visualization specialist, we must weigh the impact of the purely visual aspects of our designs as well applying visual norms that facilitate interpretation. Finally, we integrate data as the foundation of the visualization—all in a way where each coheres—that is, each contributes the same message to the viewer albeit in different languages (textual, data, interactive, and visual). It's not useful nor possible to study themes of the aesthetic, technical, and applications of visuals independently of the others.

Main Points

- Visual messages are representations of ideas and/or visual stimuli to help identify interesting patterns or events.
- The visuals are intended by the designers to be useful, and interpretable by the intended audience.
- There is a common visual language or symbols that are used to help people think to establish meaningfulness in the data.
- The meaningfulness in the data is subject to be tested—by empirical tests, by life experience, or in some particular use context, such as on the job.
- Interpreting is a cognitive act—a sustained conversation, as it were, between the viewer's mind and the visual.
- Philosophical and ethical issues attach to visualization due to the interpretation having a relationship to truthfulness.
- There is a "social norm" binding the creator and the users of the visualization.
- Both the aesthetic of visualizations and the ways people are trained to interpret them are often pegged to artistic movements.
- Computer technology is used to capture the data and prepare the data for analysis and presentation; tools for creating and using visualizations have become so popular that we must consider their roles in education, professions, and everyday life.

AESTHETICS . . . AND INFORMATION

In ancient Greek, "aesthetics" (*Αισθητική*) refers to "what the mind can perceive." The ordinary sense of aesthetics is used in several ways:

1. the study of sensations and of sentiment
2. a theory of art on the conditions of beauty
3. theories that treat the response to beauty and questions of taste
4. the study of the different forms of art

The term *aesthetic* as currently used is a synonym for beauty, or it defines what is concerned with beauty in all its accepted ways. More precisely, aesthetics is the theory of sensibilities to beauty and more particularly to artistic beauty and, by extension, the reflections on art in general. It may be employed, too, in art criticism dealing with particular works.

From its origin, the term reunites the theory of art and the theory of sensibility, as Baumgarten inaugurated in his 1750 work, *Aesthetica*, that dealt with the formation of taste and the appreciation for works of art ("Alexander Gottlieb Baumgarten," n.d.). Kant took up the theme in his *Critique of Pure Reason* (1781). Kant describes a "transcendental aesthetic," being the study of the forms that exist *a priori* to our senses of these forms, particularly time and space. For Kant, "space" refers to clarifying how intuitions are known independently of experience; "transcendental" shows how the metaphysical conclusions enrich our understanding. In his *Critique of Judgment*, the term is applied to human judgments on the appreciation of beauty.

The limits to this approach were explored by Hegel in his *Ästhetik* (Houlgate, 2016), for which aesthetic should tend toward a *science* of beauty founded upon a study of works of art. (See also Gardner's 2011 *Truth, Beauty, and Goodness Reframed*.) Questions about the interplay of the senses, reality, and truthfulness have engaged writers, philosophers, educators, and artists across domains, leading to countless theories and considerable ambivalence about how and what to study. The following cite suggests some of these stresses:

> [I]n his *Critique of Judgment*, Kant conformed to Baumgarten's new usage and employed the word aesthetic to mean the judgment of taste or the estimation of the beautiful. For Kant, an aesthetic judgment is subjective in that it relates to the internal feeling of pleasure or displeasure and not to any qualities in an external object.
>
> In 1897, Leo Tolstoy, in his *What is Art?*, criticized Baumgarten's book on aesthetics. Tolstoy opposed "Baumgarten's trinity—Good, Truth and Beauty . . ." Tolstoy asserted that "these words not only have no definite meaning, but they hinder us from giving any definite meaning to existing art." . . . Baumgarten, he said, claimed that there are three ways to know perfection: "Beauty is the perfect (the absolute) perceived by the senses. Truth is the perfect perceived by reason.

The good is the perfect attained by the moral will." Tolstoy, however, contradicted Baumgarten's theory and claimed that good, truth, and beauty have nothing in common and may even oppose each other. . . . The arbitrary uniting of these three concepts served as a basis for the astonishing theory according to which the difference between good art, conveying good feelings, and bad art, conveying wicked feelings, was totally obliterated, and one of the lowest manifestations of art, art for mere pleasure . . . came to be regarded as the highest art. And art became, not the important thing it was intended to be, but the empty amusement of idle people (*What is Art?*, VII.)

Whatever the limitations of Baumgarten's theory of aesthetics, Frederick Copleston credits him with playing a formative role in German aesthetics, extending Christian Wolff's philosophy to topics that Wolff did not consider, and demonstrating the existence of a legitimate topic for philosophical analysis that could not be reduced to abstract logical analysis." ("Alexander Gottlieb Baumgarten," n.d.)

If radical relativism can constitute a rejection for aesthetics, then an equal validity for all opinions of beauty leads to the negation of this value, the explication of a work of art based on factors *exterior* to its beauty, such as its historical context, which ruins equally the object of aesthetics and ways of interpreting it. Either way, some understanding of aesthetics remains a necessity as a foundation for our reflections on the beauty and artistic contributions of a work of art.

Hegel's "scientific" approach, and Kant's and postmodern perspectives on subjectivity in interpretation, do not remove the need for a sensibility to the contributions in visual labor, and presentation. Rather, their work and generations of writings examining their work offer us the challenge of how to balance opportunity and equality, yet provide a theoretical and practical account of truthfulness in our work that in the end legitimates the "information professions."

THE MYSTERY OF INFORMATION

Defining "information" turns out to be an astonishingly contentious activity, not least of which is because the term is vague and different camps are surprisingly possessive of their views. There are cognitivist, computer science, legal, communicative, philosophic, and myriad other, unarticulated uses by subsets of larger domains—and, of course, definitions by the everyday users. In this section, we assess some of the literatures that define information or eschew definitions.

Information Defined

I present my definition:

Information is the result of a cognitive and communicative engagement to establish meaning in otherwise static data or facts or opinions, that enable one to operate more effectively, more efficiently in one's "lifeworld," by actively/consciously accepting the reasoning behind the content in an intentionally created and purposively shared communication, regardless of physicality.

It is this definition that enflamed an anonymous reviewer and rankles partisans of the mechanistic approach. Consider some examples and questions. Why are there two phrases: "data processing" and "information processing"? Is "information" tangible, like a printed newspaper or computer file, and consequently subject to being measured and counted? Are these phrases comparable: "I count 47 subscriptions to newspapers at my library" and "I count 47 informations at my library"? Data are often counted as the number of bytes transferred in some unit of time, such as "the throughput of this device is 37GB a second." "Data" and "information" are so often treated as if they are synonyms. The cognitive and communicative properties of "processing" strongly suggest their differences.

Perhaps one source of the general lack of precision with the term information is from calculating electric impulse throughput when measuring machine performance. For instance, measuring the quality of a CPU is the speed of the number of transactions performed in a unit of time, say a second or even a nanosecond. A well-known measurement is FLOPs, or floating-point operations per second, most commonly using ANSI/IEEE Std. 754-1985; and MIPs (millions of instructions per second). (There are software- and platform-specific differences that need not detain us here.)

According to Dell EMC (2011), "EMC Corporation announced the results of the EMC-sponsored IDC Digital Universe study, 'Extracting Value from Chaos'—which found the world's information is more than doubling every two years." The disturbing part is that, as something that is not tangible and subject to traditional counting, the term "information" is used interchangeably with "data." In that sense, then, we return to the measurement of electronic activity (FLOPs or MIPs). Indeed, is human "knowledge" doubling at the same rate? The issue muddies further when terms are used more for drama than for clarity. In fact, the phrase "information doubling every two years" entered the public mind from Andy Grove, late president of Intel, referring to the number of bytes that could be transferred between computers.

Business Insider, among others, compared the mere creation of a digital file to the content of an equivalent number of printed newspapers (Aquino, 2011). It is interesting, then, that information has simultaneously different functional definitions: "amount of data" and a use comparison to a physically counted object. A significant difference appears. Anyone can shoot off a rant in an email or add comments to a blog or forward endless email chains in a blast. These documents are included in these counts of increases in "information." The careless evolution from data to information has progressed now to "knowledge" being a synonym; IndustryTap announced, "Knowledge Doubling Every 12 Months, Soon to Be Every 12 Hours" (Schilling, 2013).

A newspaper, however, is the result of (arguably) judicious selection of data (in the form of stories or the news) that is intended to be consumed by an audience. Moreover, completing the story with images, assigning authorship in the byline, and consciously selecting which stories to include by the editors add *value* to the content as well as imbuing the paper with *intentionality*. A medical practitioner masters an impressively complex and large body of "knowledge," and the practitioner exercises his or her skills combined with practical experience treating patients in selecting a plan of action for the patient. We can argue that this is knowledge because a body of "true" facts are available to someone in communication with another (the doctor to the patient), even if the communication is not oral and not even face-to-face. The medical professional understands the risks and benefits, weighs them as an expert—his or her normative role—and can explain to others his or her rationale for the decision. "Data," "information," and "knowledge" are not synonymous, but collectively enable the doctor to establish the meaningfulness of those facts to operate (no pun intended) more efficiently and effectively in his or her lifeworld.

The examples of the newspaper and the doctor introduce another facet—responsibility. A harsh commercial sense of responsibility here has legal remedy—suing for libel or for malpractice. What might exchanges with data imply?

Another take on the data/info blurring seems to be a linguistic shortcut. In the first scenario, we can imagine an office where there are untold numbers of computer files. A manager asks a staff member to locate the materials about X—in other words, to select a subset of all X that is *likely* to address yet-unasked questions about the topic X. The intentionality of presenting this subset as immediately applicable is why we drift into the use of "information"—because what we want to spend our time looking for and using should be helpful to our needs.

Breaking this activity down, the person looking to reduce the set of candidate materials decides what to include and what to exclude. There is then a form of evidence. The evidence used could be a component of the resource, such as an apt document title; or the reviewer uses his judgment of the topic to project utility *for others* by selecting the document. The evidence could be also part of the physicality of the document itself. The document may be unintelligible to the reviewer, but the physical layout of the text makes it clear that this is a legal complaint form (and that kind of document may be useful). These are all assessments of the positive aspects of the resource.

The negative ones include a range of reasons. A document titled Y may be entirely unrelated to X, and the reviewer rejects including this in the candidate set of retrieved items because she has either sufficient confidence in her decision to use the prima facie evidence; or she has knowledge of the topic sufficient to recognize the incompatibility. Another reason is that she may know or strongly believe that the recipient of these documents may reject the document for any number of reasons; or she does not wish to damage her relationship with her supervisor by appearing to be sloppy in her choices. I could argue that the reviewer rejects a potentially useful resource because she would not be able to explain or defend her choice. A response of "I don't know . . . I just grabbed it" or "the computer said so" likely would not be suitable (Uhlirova, 1996).

Casting *data*, *information*, and *knowledge* as synonyms, then lamenting "we have too much information" and that consequently we require "information trapping" suggests weirdly that the pursuit of knowledge should be restricted, that there is a right amount of knowledge or right number of facts to know. The essence of modernity and Kant is the belief in the improvement and progress of the human mind without limits.

"Information" has properties of

- intentionality;
- comprehensibility;
- something that can be communicated to others;
- evidence of suitability for some purpose;
- responsibility;
- suggestions of suitability for another person or persons;
- reflexivity—the choice of the data for the purpose reflects on the reviewer/ selector and between the reviewer and the consumer;
- social context—awareness of unarticulated, immeasurable aspects, the "lifeworld," that impacts decision making;
- cognition—requiring active, conscious thought, not passive receipt, for acceptability.

. . . Otherwise they're just data.

OTHER PERSPECTIVES ON INFORMATION

The need for a better sense of what information is, and perhaps what it is not, is demonstrated convincingly by recent monographs, articles, academic groups, and special editions on the philosophy of information.

There is no dominant perspective, but several streams of thought have emerged. One is Floridi's *Philosophy of information* (2011). His argument is not supportive of the communicative rationality point of view; take a glance at his works (e.g., see http://www.philosophyofinformation.net/).

Other streams seem to regard information from the view of postmodernist theory. Writ large, postmodernists eschew the issue of "truth," and truthfulness, and favor the relativistic, social construction of knowledge. The foundation of these points of view is that social institutions are systems of inclusion and of exclusion. While the original expressions of this view of the West—Lyotard, Derrida, and the first wave of postmodernists—lead to our (hopefully improved) views of gender, race, and inclusion, I question here whether the perspective may have ossified: the perspective is viewed as dogma, hence off-limits for investigation, and as a necessarily true fact, and so useless to question. If so, then can there be any evolution of the ideas? Is there possibility of examination of the theories and products of those theories if there is no self-reflection? In the InfoVis environment, the purpose is all about exposing unanticipated relationships that suggest new knowledge . . . only a researcher or practitioner open to exploring uncomfortable leads from the data, wherever they may lead, might benefit society.

There is no single undeniable theory of knowledge, or meaning construction, or interactions with others and institutions. Each of the many theories about knowledge and interpretation contribute to our understanding. An acknowledged perspective by an author, pointing out immediately his or her frame of interpretation, as Eagleton (1988) does in "The Ideology of the Aesthetic," allows us to contextualize his message. In this way the variability of interpretations is somewhat better supported, or "legitimized," because there is a chain of the message's intentionality, evidence of some purpose for the writing of the book, self-reflection, and purpose of the application of his ideas.

HOW DO THESE STREAMS FLOW TOGETHER?

My thesis is that visual literacy is now well-addressed outside the visual arts area. The typical citizen reading a paper or searching online enjoys the power of the graphics and may take away a prima facie interpretation of the data. Interactive "information" visualizations are purposefully created by someone or a group of someones *with the intention* that the result of their labor be interpretable, truthful (in that the visual representation of the data does not deceive the viewer), and designed to allow the viewer to investigate for him- or herself the underlying data sources ("details on demand") as well as being able to explore the justification in the design that creates unanticipated relationships in the data (the statistical level created when preparing the data for visualization).

The intersection of theories of interpretation, accountability, truthfulness, equality of participation, institutional practices, and aesthetics flow together in a "post-postmodern" multicultural world (Kirby, 2006; Benson & Stangroom, 2006; Putnam, 2002).

INFOVIS AS COMMUNICATIVE EVENT

Information visualization displays meet the definition of an art form in that there is an *intended* message to be communicated, and the *principles of graphic design* are applied as they are in other information graphics. Unlike other forms of representational art, InfoVis *is* a representational art of "information" as an abstract phenomenon, with the goal of engaging the viewer with forms of interactivity that are not possible with a painting. Plato laments that a "painting goes on saying the same thing," referring to his belief that truth, utility, and understanding are impossible without a means of querying the person responsible for the message in art; Hegel suggests contextualizing a painting to help us understand more about the painting, the artist, and society. But the digital painting (as it were) has immediacy. Unique in the arts, perhaps, interactive information visualization requires engagement in real-time (addressing Kant's issue about time), and an interface as a malleable medium of ever-improving screen resolution, because the visual toolkit used cognitively by the viewer to understand the visualization is the same toolkit used by the creators of a visualization (addressing space and *a priori* issues). Perhaps even more astonishing is that an InfoVis combines the "kinetic potential" of discovering new facts, or at least curious relationships suggested by the data, and a form of warrant that encourages relativistic interpretations, providing the data and algorithms behind the data offer transparency on the creators' part. Consequently, there is the potential for real "communication" between the viewer and the creator; between the viewers and other viewers and, by extension with society at large. Interactive information visualization may well approach critical theorist Jürgen Habermas's "ideal speech situation" (a most useful, if not necessarily achievable, aspiration) in which instrumental use of (visual) language by one party may be defeated in favor of the kind of "goal-directedness" in which parties work together to establish meaningfulness, with liberty to question any perspective, to ask for and to receive an answer to another's claims about truthfulness in their speech, actions, or visualizations (Benoît, 1998, 2014, 2015, 2016).

REFERENCES

Alexander Gottlieb Baumgarten. (n.d.) In *Wikipedia.* Retrieved September 26, 2018, from https://en.wikipedia.org/wiki/Alexander_Gottlieb_Baumgarten.

Aquino, J. (2011, February 15). Scientists calculate how much information there is in the world: 295 EXABYTES. *Business Insider.* Retrieved from https://www.businessinsider.com/amount-of-information-in-the-world-2011-2

Benoît, G. (1998). Information seeking as communicative action. Unpublished PhD dissertation, University of California, Los Angeles.

Benoît, G. (2014). The aesthetic turn: Thoughts about knowledge claims of information visual systems. *Preservation, Digital Technology & Culture 43*(2), 100-113. doi 10.115 /pdtc-2014-0003.

Benoît, G. (2015). Visual communication as an information activity. *Journal of Visual Literacy, 34*(2), 51–67.

Benoît, G. (2016, September). The "beautiful" in information: Thoughts about visual literacy and aesthetics. *Journal of Visual Literacy, 35*(1), 60–78.

Benson, O., & Stangroom, J. (2006). *Why truth matters.* London: Continuum.

Castro, N. (2008). *Slide:ology.* Sebastopol, CA: O'Reilly.

Dell EMC. (2011, June 28). World data more than doubling every two years—driving big data opportunity, new IT roles. Retrieved from https://www.emc.com/about/news /press/2011/20110628-01.htm

Eagleton, T. (1988). The ideology of the aesthetic. *Poetics Today 9*(2), pp. 327-338. http:// shelleycampbell.weebly.com/uploads/9/8/7/7/9877175/eagleton_the_ideology_of_ the_aesthetic.pdf.

Floridi, L. (2011). *Philosophy of information.* Oxford: Oxford University Press.

Habermas, J. (1984). *Theory of communicative action.* Boston, MA: Beacon.

Hegel, G. W. F. (rep. 1985). *Einleitung in der Ästhetik.* München: Fink.

Houlgate, S. (2016), "Hegel's Aesthetics." In Edward N. Zalta (ed.), *Stanford Encyclopedia of Philosophy Archive.* Retrieved from https://plato.stanford.edu/archives/spr2016 /entries/hegel-aesthetics/

Kant, I. (1790/1914). *Critique of judgment.* (*Kritik der Urteilskraft*) (J. H. Bernard, Trans.). London: Macmillan.

Kant, I. (1781). *Kritik der reinen Vernunft* [Critique of Pure Reason]. Riga: Hartnoch.

Kirby, A. (2006). The death of postmodernism and beyond. https://philosophynow.org /issues/58/The_Death_of_Postmodernism_And_Beyond.

Knight, W. (2017, July 12). Biased algorithms are everywhere, and no one seems to care. *MIT Technology Review.* Retrieved from https://www.technologyreview .com/s/608248/biased-algorithms-are-everywhere-and-no-one-seems-to-care/.

Krug, S. (2014). *Don't make me think, revisited: A common sense approach to web and mobile usability* (3rd ed.). San Francisco, CA: New Riders.

Plato. (1995). *Phaedrus.* (Woodruff, Trans.) Indianapolis, IN: Hackett.

Putnam, H. (2002). *The collapse of the fact/value dichotomy and other essays.* Cambridge, MA: Harvard University Press.

Schilling, D. (2013). Knowledge doubling every 12 months, soon to be every 12 hours. IndustryTap. Retrieved from http://www.industrytap.com/knowledge-doubling-every-12 -months-soon-to-be-every-12-hours/3950

Uhlířová, L. (1994). On the role of the PC as a relevant object in face-to-face communication. *Journal of Pragmatics, 22*(5), 511–27.

## CHAPTER 3

The Art of Information Visualization

Perhaps a better title for this chapter would be the "Artistry of Information Visualization." While lots of applications will present data in an attractive format, the artistry of InfoVis requires that we understand the design principles that enable communication between the designers, the data, and the viewers of the final interactive graphic.

We review just a few fundamentals of graphic design. Naturally it wouldn't be wise to attempt all of the graphic principles in a single reading. Nevertheless there are some common principles that will facilitate communicating with graphic designers and be a bridge between the aesthetics of visualization and data.

The fundamentals include typography, color theory, and composition. The approach to each of these differs significantly between the graphic designer and the computer programmer (Hartley, 2017; Polgar, 2017). The former builds on the rich history of visual communication and languages, with all the craftsmanship one expects of an expert. With concomitant skills, the latter codifies the representation into a version suited for computers. Presenting data to be interpreted, to be explored, to be felt viscerally and emotionally requires a dedication to truthful representations of the data, encouraged by the appropriate graphic representation for the experience. We seek a coherence between the viewers' aesthetic experience expressed through our choice of composition, typography, and color, and the sense of the data to facilitate explanation, exploration, and exposure of new, interesting events.

COMPOSITION

Around the world, history demonstrates abiding efforts to systematize the structure of art and proportions of beauty. Seemingly every ancient culture left signs of its integration of mathematics with nature to create objects and images of beauty. As early as the sixth century in China the "square script" (figure 3.1) was created to be easy for the layperson to master (Nanyang Technical University, 2017). By systematizing the stroke order in a square frame, with eight inner triangular areas, writing became easier to learn, to critique, and to share the aesthetic experience of writing across the Sui and Tang dynasties (Zhao & Baldauf, 2008). The result was "scholar-officials"—men who demonstrated vast knowledge of literature, calligraphy, religion, morals, and ethics, who were tested repeatedly to become powerful officials of the state (Metropolitan Museum of Art, 2004).

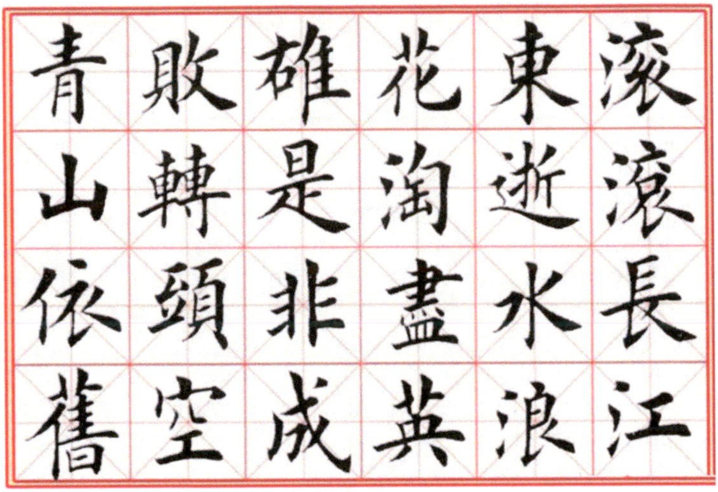

青	敗	碓	花	東	滾
山	轉	是	淘	逝	滾
依	頭	非	盡	水	長
舊	空	成	英	浪	江

FIGURE 3.1 Early example of systematizing ideographs to facilitate learning and reading. *https://blogs.ntu.edu.sg/hss-language -evolution/wiki/chapter-17/*

The powerful effects of systematizing how to create and how to read visual arts cannot be understated.

Perhaps a most famous example is the ancient Greeks' golden mean, or golden ratio (figure 3.2; Livio, 2002). This is a proportion between parts of a whole image where one part is in proportion to the other part, leading to a ratio of 1:1.618 (actually 1.6180339887). The ratio of a box with proportions *b:c* to *a:b* is the same as *a:b* to *a:d*. The same ratio can be expressed in as a logarithmic spiral. Both these expressions of proportion find physical and artistic expression in all fields of graphic and architectural work.

Swiss-French architect Le Corbusier (1887–1965) incorporated the spiral version of the golden mean in some of his architecture. Like many modernists, he echoed the naturalist tendencies of Renaissance artists/craftsmen, such as Albrecht Dürer (1471–1528) or Leonardo DaVinci (1452–1519)—modeling their technical work (Greek *technē, τέχνη,* or man-made craft) on proportions of nature (Moulis, 2010), very often on the proportions of the human body (figures 3.3A, 3.3B, and 3.4).

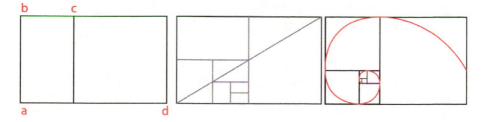

bc:ab = ab:ad

golden mean, 1:1.618   equidistant divisions

spiral version of the

golden mean, 1:1.618

FIGURE 3.2 Early Greek systemization of proportions in a conscious pursuit for "beauty." *Courtesy of the author*

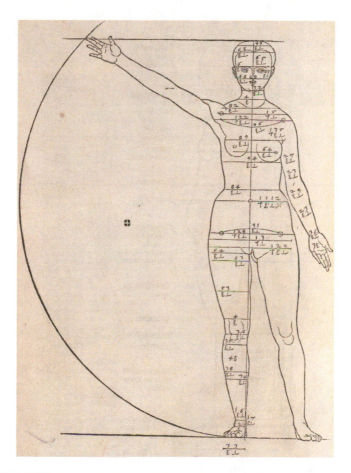

FIGURE 3.3A Systemization of design using "natural" proportions based on the human body. Proportion study of a woman, from the front. Albrecht Dürer (1471–1528), Hieriñ sind begriffen vier Bücher von menschlicher Proportion, 1528. *FA 6470.202, Houghton Library, Harvard University. Public domain; FA 6470.202, Houghton Library, Harvard University*

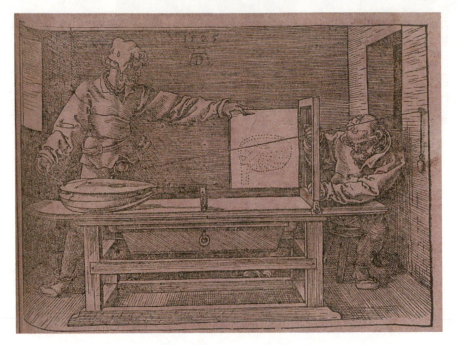

FIGURE 3.3B "Geometrie & Perspektive & Instrument," Der Zeichner der Laute—
Instrumentelle Methode zur Herstellung eines zentralperspektivischen Bildes.
Public domain; Deutsche Fotothek

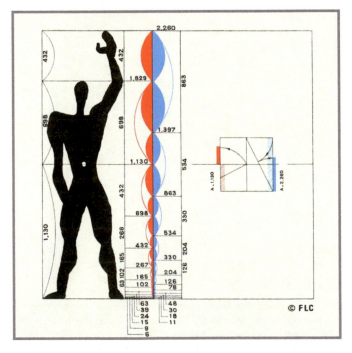

FIGURE 3.4 Le Corbusier, Humanité, 1945.Le Corbusier's Humanité guide based
on human proportions. *https://www.amazon.fr/Modulor-2-Fondation-Corbusier
/dp/3764361883*

The industry of graphics has settled on a handful of principles that facilitate graphic production. I see the trend deriving from the end days of German modernism (Heller & Fili, 1998), around the 1930s, and settling in as a standard for graphic production after Müller-Brockmann's 1996 *Grid Systems in Graphic Design* (figure 3.5), coincidentally bolstered by the rise of the computer's monitor's *x, y* coordinate grid (Lunenfeld, 2000). (The reader will forgive the extreme reductionism of identifying a single movement among countless that influence our visual topography.) By the end of this movement, around the 1930s, the style of the day had developed from a highly symmetrical, floral-oriented design toward larger main elements, smaller color pallet, and the idea of repeating a visual theme . . . but repeating it either in tremendous quantity or by reducing it to a sequence of three (Meggs & Purvis, 2016). The *Plakatstil* (poster style) returned to Western design motifs in the 1960s, 1970s, and early 1980s, in American posters, of which the posters of David Lance Goines may be most iconic. It is arguable that the principles of design, derived from modernism and promulgated in the revival of posters and mathematical models of typography design, establish the visual topology and typography we adopt unthinkingly.

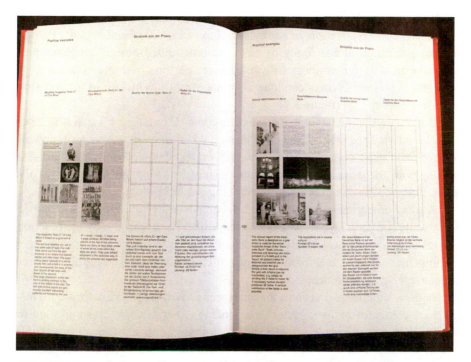

FIGURE 3.5 Müller-Brockmann's Grid System dominates and guides contemporary visual expectations. *http://olympiagraphics.com/wp-content/uploads/grid-systems -img-3.jpg*

When teaching design composition for posters and for websites, there are some introductory rules based on the above discussion. One is the "rule of thirds." This equates to (no more than) three colors in the design, three typefaces, and three display areas in a design composition (figure 3.6).

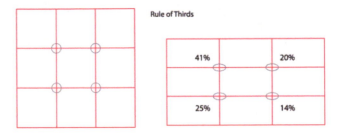

FIGURE 3.6 The rule of thirds (left), and applied to a screen design (right). The numbers show the percentages of where people scan first when reading an image. *https://www.interaction-design.org/literature/article/the-rule-of-thirds-know-your -layout-sweet-spots*

The computational ease of design and replication exerts long-studied impact on theories of interpretation, of reality and simulacra, and of authenticity. Perhaps the popularization and ubiquity of easy computer-aided design templates have helped restrain design mashups with an easy and personalized rule of three.

Other common layouts combine examples from the history of art and from modern poster design (figure 3.7).

Having determined a framework for the composition, the next step is to determine how to tell the story of the data through the placement, shape, size, and differences, to form a coherent, visually attractive, and data-appropriate layout. As a starting point, here are some common approaches, knowing the design will evolve as we integrate the data, user needs, and computer technology.

A trend emerging in InfoVis favors a composite design. Figures 3.8 and 3.9 show some common layouts where the composition is driven first by the functionality of the graphic area. Usually these designs have three major functional areas: a graphic, user control panel for interacting with the data, and a graphic display area, exposing the details on demand.

In these functional divisions, the main area is used for the visualization. These graphics consist of realistic images, recognizable maps, icons, drawings, and for abstractions particularly, a set of visual primitives (dot, line, square, rectangle, circle) that are akin to words (semantic elements). Their composition parallels syntax. Together they start the "visual storytelling." Recently both business and research articles have turned to the idea of storytelling, or using visuals to communicate with others. Systems analysts and other technical fields have long relied on imagery ranging from highly complex network and data flows to icon-laden simplifications, called user system diagrams, that introduce new ideas to non-technical staff (Knaflic, 2015).

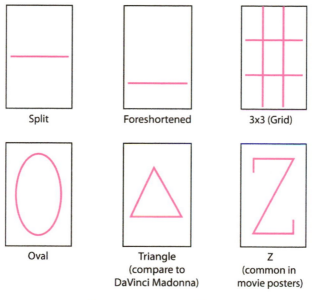

Common poster/graphic layouts

FIGURE 3.7 Common poster layouts. *Courtesy of the author*

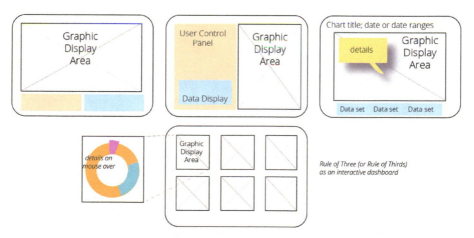

FIGURE 3.8 Common contemporary layouts for information visualization. *Courtesy of the author*

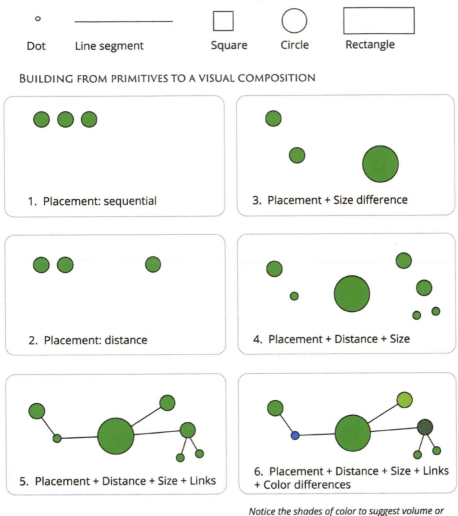

BASIC SHAPES ["VISUAL PRIMITIVES"]

Dot   Line segment   Square   Circle   Rectangle

BUILDING FROM PRIMITIVES TO A VISUAL COMPOSITION

1. Placement: sequential

2. Placement: distance

3. Placement + Size difference

4. Placement + Distance + Size

5. Placement + Distance + Size + Links

6. Placement + Distance + Size + Links + Color differences

Notice the shades of color to suggest volume or strength of association; complementary colors in the same graphic element suggest similarities but significant differents.

FIGURE 3.9 From a small vocabulary of visual semantics ("primitives"), we construct a visual sentence by adjusting the visual syntax: sequence, size differences, distance; associating links and clusters to aid interpretation. *Courtesy of the author*

Weighing the functional areas of the design is helped by practicing decomposing and critiquing existing designs (figure 3.10).

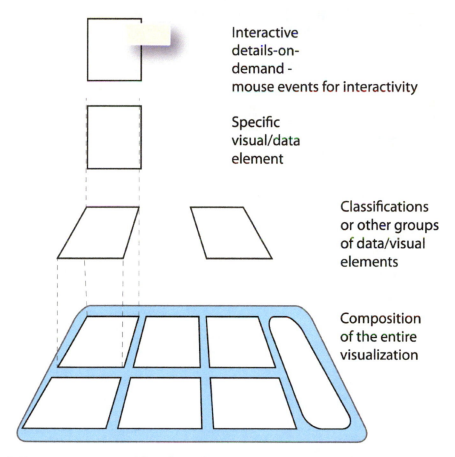

Interactive details-on-demand - mouse events for interactivity

Specific visual/data element

Classifications or other groups of data/visual elements

Composition of the entire visualization

FIGURE 3.10 Decomposition of an information visualization. On the left appear functional regions of the graph; on the right, a long "control panel" to host interactive controls (checkboxes, sliders). *Courtesy of the author*

VISUAL ELEMENTS

Next, we consider a systematic listing of placement and critique that ensures we have reviewed composition contributors to the story of the data.

- Unity/Harmony
  - *Proximity*: sensible spacing between elements
  - *Similarity*: repeating an element with other similar ones
  - *Continuity*: prolonging a line or pattern
  - *Repetition*: copying items or units repeatedly
  - *Rhythm*: successful when a position, size, or recurrent color as well as the use of a graphic element have a central point of interruption

Repeated pattern of same primitives

Repeated pattern of same primitives;
single item with color difference

Repeated pattern of same primitives;
single element with a different shape

Combined repeated pattern + single element
with a different shape + single element with
color difference

Adding interactivity: mouseover for details-on-demand

Dept: Administration
Budget: $1,400,000
Overrun: Comp. Equip.
% over: 150%

FIGURE 3.11 Systematic review of patterns, color, placement, and source data. *Courtesy of the author*

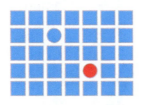

Unity / Harmony

FIGURE 3.12 Unity/harmony of positioning visual elements. *Courtesy of the author*

- Equilibrium
  - *Symmetry*: elements on each side of the axes are positioned in a symmetrical fashion
  - *Asymmetry*: elements on each side have a different shape but create a visual equilibrium
  - *Circularity*: elements are positioned to create a circular form

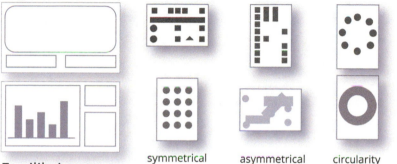

Equilibrium

symmetrical   asymmetrical   circularity

designprinciples2.ai

FIGURE 3.13 Assembling design areas based on principles of symmetry/asymmetry. *Courtesy of the author*

- Hierarchy
  - *Tree structure*: elements are ordered according to a structure with a root/trunk, branches, and sub-branches
  - *Parent-child relationship*: elements are distributed among themselves in a parent-child relationship
  - *Size*: elements of the same thickness belong to the same hierarchical position class

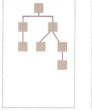    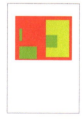

tree   parent/child   deondogram   force-directed   tree (another kind)
[provided there's
a context for an
hierarchical description]

Hierarchical

FIGURE 3.14 Various trees and equilibrium designs + color. *Courtesy of the author*

FIGURE 3.15 Graphic examples of representing hierarchies of data relationship. *Courtesy of the author*

- Scale/Proportion
  - *Size*: elements of different sizes are related to each other
  - *Ratio*: elements are linked by a ratio, creating a visual harmony
  - *Divisions*: multiple focal points for the elements, creating a sense of composition

- Dominance/Accenting
  - *Highlighting*: breaking the visual hierarchy by using a different shape to accentuate an item
  - *Color*: distinguish an element from a series of similar forms
  - *Size*: the elements have different sizes, permitting the reader/viewer to focus on a particular part of the visual story

- Similarity/Contrast
  - *Lightness/shadow*: a clear separation between the foreground and background, contrasting the elements
  - *lines/shapes*: varying the texture and forms of the visual elements ("visual primitives") to effect a contrast

We tell the story of the data through our choices of these design elements and their construction—their placement within and among each other.

TYPOGRAPHY

Typography has been subjected to similar attempts at systematization. Returning to the Dürer example, we see his mapping of letter forms to the human form. The French seventeenth-century *Imprimerie royale* (later *impériale*) applied a grid system to establish a logical model for print (figs. 3.16 and 3.17). Today, arguably, the most influential type systemization is from the *Neue Typographie* movement (Tschichold, 1928), motivating the International Style of the 1960s, perhaps culminating in modernist and postmodern typefaces, such as Univers (Adrian Frutiger, 1954) and the ubiquitous Helvetica font (designed by Max Miedinger and Eduard Hoffman, 1957). By adjusting the width and angle like a math problem, typefaces can be manipulated quickly into various font widths (bold, condensed, black, ultra-condensed; not unlike the MultipleMaster digital font format).

But note that contemporary font files include the entire history of typography—from traditional book fonts such as Garamond and Jenson, Caslon and Trajan, to modern representations and recuts such as Myriad Pro, Gill California, and the various Garamond recuts, as well as modern ligatures, increasing the aesthetic possibilities.

FIGURE 3.16 Renaissance systemization of typography: Dürer's "Of the just shaping of letters." *https://www.gutenberg.org /files/37103/37103-h/37103-h.htm*

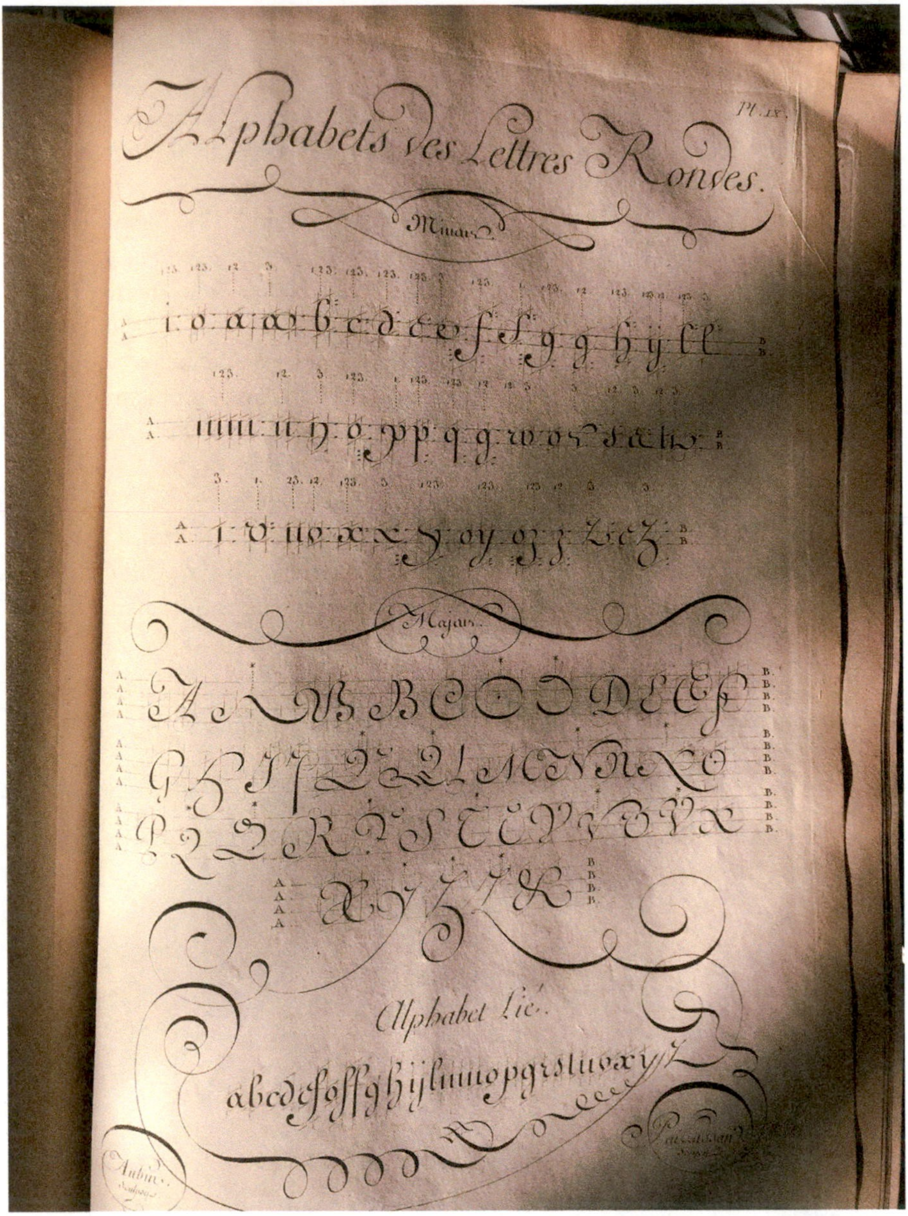

FIGURE 3.17 Systematizing the teaching of writing, from Diderot and d'Alembert's Encyclopédie, Paris, 1751. *Courtesy of the author*

Three Fonts . . .

The rule of thirds applies to fonts, too.

The use of fonts is more subtle than one might imagine at first glance. The extreme subtlety of detail when designing fonts contributes to an equally subtle affective impact on a design. The choice of fonts also contributes more evidently to legibility. To a graphic designer, the choice of font contributes to the overall design, addressing more than legibility because the design is tempered with sensitivity to the limitations of the output device (monitor), size of the font, and the overall aesthetic tone.

Does this matter in InfoVis? Indeed, it does! Experience shows that both neophyte designers of visualizations and commercial visualization applications often overlook the role that type plays in legibility, aesthetics, and meaning construction. Yet the most successful visualizations are those where the details of data, design, and aesthetics are in harmony, and the interactivity allows the end user to understand the explanation and to explore.

Turning back to fonts in our designs, the rule of three applies to the choice of typography, too. In design practice, there is usually a heading font, body text, and then a font for details. For instance, we might choose Avenir Next Bold for a title, Avenir Next for the body text (not bold, to be a second font), and Garamond for details, the third (figure 3.18). Even though two of the roles (title and body) are the same font name, one is bold and the other is regular. This equates to two fonts. It is common, too, to use a serif font for a title and then a sans serif for the other two (or vice versa). Learning which fonts to use comes only from practice and studying examples. Figures 3.18 to 3.22 represent application of the rule of three to type, underscoring the heading or title font, subtitle, and body font styles. Figure 3.19 shows Chinese fonts, while figures 3.20 to 3.22 are all interpretations of the same message in Arabic. Each varies by the choice of title, subtitle, and body text styles.

There are many websites that demonstrate trends in taste about types and make useful comparisons. Visit these commercial and popular sites for examples: Monotype (https://www.monotype.com/blog/), typeconnection (http://www.typeconnection.com/matches.php), Typewolf, a favorite (https://www.typewolf.com), and Just My Type (https://justmytype.co). For a fun historical review, see 99designs (https://99designs.com/blog/design-history-movements/history-of-digital-fonts/), and for a complete web-oriented manual, see the Web Style Guide (http://webstyleguide.com/wsg3/8-typography/4-web-typefaces.html). Given that our visualizations may be web-based, it is a pleasant adventure to visit web fonts (.woff) to see how they may work in your computing environment (https://www.w3schools.com/howto/howto_google_fonts.asp).

Because there is a vast literature sharing the beauty of typography, it would be a foolish enterprise to attempt to describe all things typographic in this context. It is nevertheless useful to share a few fundamental terms for describing type. Readers are encouraged to explore the wonderful world of type online and in print.

Headline
Subhead

Sed ut perspiciatis unde omnis iste natus error sit voluptatem accusantium doloremque laudantium, totam rem aperiam, eaque ipsa quae ab illo inventore veritatis et quasi architecto beatae vitae dicta sunt explicabo. Nemo enim ipsam voluptatem quia voluptas sit aspernatur

Avenir Bold
Avenir Regular

Garamond

FIGURE 3.18 The headline and subhead are sans serif fonts to emphasize legibility from a distance; the body text is a popular serif, Garamond, for attractive reading up close. *Courtesy of the author*

标题或横幅字体

副标题类型

(a)

这是用于文本排版的传统方法或流行方法的示例。中文出版物中使用了许多类型的面孔，每个出版社都有自己的风格。但这里的重点是展示一个吸引人的，引人注目的标题，一个稍微适度的小标题，然后是一个非常清晰的正文。

(b)

使用历史书法的标题

副标题类型

此示例仅用于演示不同的字体。人们认识到，这里没有代表的设计史。目的是只显示"三分法"可能适用于当今的数字环境。台湾，中国和其他中国地区的字体选择似乎有所不同。我们在信息可视化领域的主要兴趣是最终用户理解图像，数据和文本的关系。

FIGURE 3.19 Two layout traditions: horizontal and vertical text. In (a) the text, like figure 3.18, uses a highly legible sans serif version of simplified Chinese. A traditional vertical layout is shown in (b). The traditional feeling of this design is supported by the display font, square or clerical writing. *Courtesy of the author*

مثال لقاعدة الثلث في اللغة العربية

علــى ســبــيــل الــمــثــال ، نــجــرب الــكــوفــية

يجب أن يكون نص النص مقروءًا وجذابًا ويساهم في النغمة العامة للوثيقة. يؤدي استخدام محرف شائع يـسـتـنـد إلـى الـكـمـبـيـوتـر ، مـثـل هـذا الـنـوع ، إلـى تـحـسـيـن الـوضـوح. يعد كل من "ثولوث" و "الكوفي" خطين جميلين للغاية على الطراز التقليدي. يمكن لأجهزة الكمبيوتر اليوم تـكـرار هـذه الـأنـواع وتـوفـيـر مـجـمـوعـة مـن الـأسـالـيـب الـحـديـثـة للـاخـتـيـار مـن بـيـنـهـا.

FIGURE 3.20 Example of the rule of three for Arabic; Naskh is the title and Kufic, a traditional style, is displayed in a stretched style, Kashida. *Courtesy of the author*

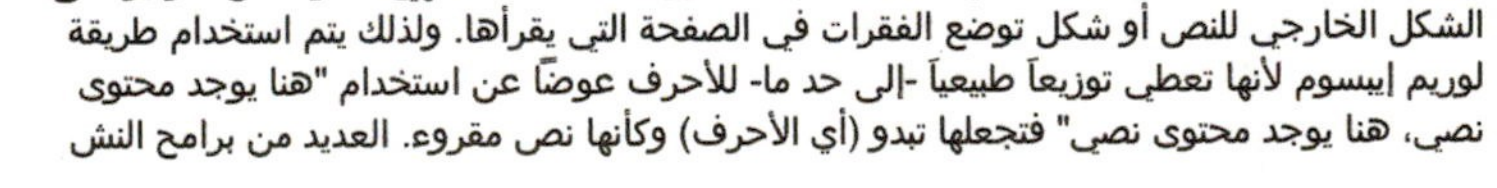

خط العنوان نمط الكتابة اليدوية التقليدية الجميلة

الخط التقليدي للعنوان الفرعي

ناك حقيقة مثبتة منذ زمن طويل وهي أن المحتوى المقروء لصفحة ما سيلهي القارئ عن التركيز على الشكل الخارجي للنص أو شكل توضع الفقرات في الصفحة التي يقرأها. ولذلك يتم استخدام طريقة لوريم إيسوم لأنها تعطي توزيعاً طبيعياً -إلى حد ما- للأحرف عوضًا عن استخدام "هنا يوجد محتوى نصي، هنا يوجد محتوى نصي" فتجعلها تبدو (أي الأحرف) وكأنها نص مقروء. العديد من برامج النش

FIGURE 3.21 Here the tone of the graphic is shifted by using Tuluth, considered a very beautiful style, for the title and retreating from the stretched style of the Square Kufic, lessening the stateliness of the graphic. *Courtesy of the author*

العنوان الرئيسي

مثال على ذلك باستخدام أساليب الخط التقليدي الجميل

يجب أن يكون نص النص واضحًا بشكل واضح ، سواء كان معروضًا على جهاز كمبيوتر أو عند الطباعة على ملصق بالطبع هناك تقاليد مختلفة في الفن الثقافي والرسمي في العالم الناطق بالعربية. هذه المظاهرة هي في المقام الأول لوضع مواز بين قاعدة الثلث والطباعة على الكمبيوتر.

لم يصل الخط إلى ما هو عليه الآن إلا بعد أن مر بأربع مراحل، الأول: الدور الصوري المادي، الثاني: الدور الصوري المعنوي، الثالث: الدور الصوري الحرفي، الرابع: الدور الحرقي الصَّرْف. قضى الإنسان قرونًا عديدة لا يعرف الكتابة لاستغنائه عنها لما كان فيه من بساطة العيش، ولمّا اتجه الإنسان نحو المدنية بدأ في التعبير عن أفكاره واحتياجاته بالرسم، وهي الكتابة الصورية، وأشهر هذه الصور هي الكتابة الهيروغليفية.

جميع الخطوط المتداولة في العالم ترجع في أصلها إلى قسمين كبيرين، الأول: الخط اليوناني القديم، ومنه تَوَلَّد الخط الروماني والسلاڤي والقوطي، ومن هذه تفرعت خطوط لغات أوروبا. الثاني: الخط الشرقي، والمراد به الخطوط المستعملة في كتابة اللغات الشرقية، كالخط العربي والسرياني والكلداني والعبراني والحبشي والهندي والصيني، ويدخل تحت هذا القسم اللغات الشرقية القديمة: كالجِمْيري والنَّبطي والكوفي والسامري والأسفيني. من هذه الخطوط ماهو مستقل في منشأه كالصيني والأسفيني، أما بقية الخطوط فترجع إلى أصل واحد وهو الآرمي، وقد كان مستخدمًا عند الآشوريين، وهم دولة كانت تسكن آشور وبابل، وكانت كتابتهم تُعرف بالكتابة الإسفينية أو المسمارية. تفرّع من هذا الخط الحرف النبطي وهو أصل الخط العربي النسخي، وقد سمي نبطيًا لأنه كان مستخدمًا عند النبطيين في مدن بصرى وحوران؛ وقد عَثَر الباحثون في تلك الجهات وغيرها على نوعين مختلفين من الكتابة، أحدهما أقرب إلى الكتابة الآرمية وهو الأقدم، والآخر أقرب إلى الخط العربي المعروف.

يعود أصل الكتابة المعروفة الآن إلى وادي النيل بشكل الصور الهيروغليفية، ثم حولها الفينيقيون إلى حروف هجائية، وعلموها اليونانين في القرن السادس عشر قبل الميلاد؛ ثم انتقلت للآشوريين بعد ذلك، وعرفت بالحرف الآرمي، ومن الحرف الآرمي أُشتقت الخطوط التي تُكتب بها اللغات الشرقية، وأكثرها انتشارًا الخط العربي.[10]

FIGURE 3.22 Here the title is assigned the noble Square Kufic, as one might in the West select a bold style. *Courtesy of the author*

Type Classification

The major division between fonts is serif and sans serif; after this, the categories of type really vary. There is no universally adopted standardized description of all types, but within the two major divisions there are convenient groupings. Some computerized fonts are copies of earlier handmade type designs (or book faces).

There are also modern reinterpretations of book faces, that is, slight modifications of traditional designs to accommodate new technologies, such as new printing presses and, of course, the computer.

COLOR

Color sets the tone and expectations of what we view as much as it impacts legibility and cognition (Isenberg, 2014). It follows that when designing an information visualization it is important to reflect on our color choices. Most commercial products, however great they may be for data analysis and facilitating creating useful charts, do not allow the end user to control the choice of color or the composition of the final product. The emphasis of these products seems to be to remove the challenge of *creating* a visualization in order to focus on the data. Yet for our purposes, a designer of a really successful visualization understands the application of color as a contributor to interpretation and a guide for the user. Equally, the designer knows how to explain the limitations of powerful commercial tools when the colors are assigned automatically by the application.

As we have already noted, the use of color and a lighter hue of a color helps end users see degrees of strength and degrees of relationship between graphic elements and the surface image of the underlying data. But what is even more interesting is that, computationally, we can manipulate the color expression by the computer to reflect easily these relationships and the data. For example, imagine we are using the color red to demonstrate a group of shared data. A lighter hue of red is used to suggest a relationship among visual elements, but with a less strong bond. The color red is represented by the software as in the RGBA model (red green blue alpha) as rgba(255, 0, 0, 1). The values range from 0 to 255, to create 256 total discrete values. A lighter shade is rgba(255, 204, 204, 1). Notice that we can map the data that shows the relationship to the *visual expression* of that relationship, and do so easily in the code we use to create the visualization. Imagine, then, that as an end user offers other input, the relationship of the data may change and we can easily update the rgba colors to reflect those changes in the data. A knowing integration of the user input, the data being updated in response, and the visualization recalculating its color values demonstrates the kind of tight unity of the whole for really engaging the end user.

For a monochromatic color scheme, figure [data + color model] we cycle through data values using a script. We can alter the color opacity as a way of reflecting the increasing value of the underlying data. For instance, say we have a dataset consisting of an array mydata = (10, 20, 05, 100). For each data value, we change the color (e.g., 10% opacity, 20%, . . . 100%):

```
    while j < len(mydata) {
            opacityOfData = mydata[j] * .01;
            // e.g., 10 * .01 = 0.01; 100 & .01 = 1.0
            // this creates rgba(200, 200, 200, opacityOfData)

    }
```

Some visualization texts focus on the biological aspects of color and vision. As we age, the retina's sensitivity to color changes. Our eyes become less responsive to color in the blue range, shifting the interpretation of the color toward yellow. Color there raises questions about the suitability of screen designs, messages, and signage, and provides an extra basis for evaluating the suitability and effectiveness of our color choices. From the theories of color we have several standards to describe a "color space," among them, primary/secondary/tertiary colors, and complementary/analogous.

- Primary colors: red, green, blue.
- Secondary: green, orange, purple.
- Tertiary: yellow-orange, red-orange, red-purple, blue-purple, blue-green, yellow green.
- Adding white to any color creates the "tint"; adding black, the "shade"; gray creates the "tone."

When considering color pallet, besides the affective and aesthetic question, the data themselves contribute to the choice. In figure 3.23 the data to be displayed are binary (yes|no, 0|1), in categories, sequential, and combinations. For each data example, there is a color pallet consisting of monochromatic, complementary, analogous, and high-contrast versions.

Choice of Color Pallets

Graphic designers of print materials rely on the Pantone Matching System (PMS) for precise identification of colors for their work. PMS applies, too, in computing settings. Adobe Illustrator (now part of Adobe Creative Cloud) provides the user with colors expressed as PMS, rgb, hue-saturation-brightness, and hexadecimal triplets (e.g., #ff0000). This means the designer using these tools easily understands the computationally based expression of color. Yet the designer still must consider the tone of color that supports the desired aesthetic tone of the visualized topic.

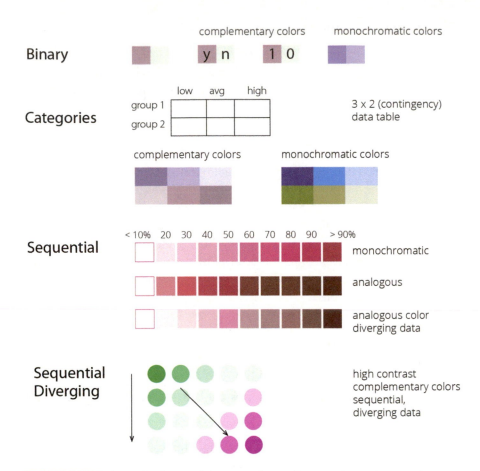

FIGURE 3.23 Data and color models: monochromatic, complementary, analogous, and contrast. *Courtesy of the author*

Online we find many guides, such as Canva (https://www.canva.com /learn/100-color-combinations/) for combinations and Palleton (http://paletton .com) for helping us identify color combinations according to a variety of computer codes and demonstrations.

REFERENCES

Hartley, S. (2017). *The fuzzy and the techie: Why the liberal arts will rule the digital world.* New York, NY: Houghton Mifflin Harcourt.

Heller, S., & Fili, L. (1998). *German modernism: Graphic design from Wilhelm to Weimar.* San Francisco, CA: Chronicle Books.

Isenberg, T. (2014). Information visualization: Perception and color. Retrieved April 25, 2018, from http://www.aviz.fr/wiki/uploads/Teaching2014/iv2014_color-perception .pdf

Knaflic, C. N. (2015). *Storytelling with data: A data visualization guide for business professionals.* New York, NY: Wiley.

Livio, M. (2002). *The golden ratio: The story of phi, the world's most astonishing number.* New York, NY: Broadway Publ.

Lunenfeld, P. (2000). *Snap to grid.* Cambridge, MA: MIT Press.

Meggs, P. B., & Purvis, A. W. (2016). *Meggs' history of graphic design* (6th ed.). New York, NY: Wiley.

Metropolitan Museum of Art. (2004, October). Scholar-officials of China. Retrieved from https://www.metmuseum.org/toah/hd/schg/hd_schg.htm

Moulis, A. (2010). Forms and techniques: Le Corbusier, the spiral plan and diagram architecture. *Architectural Research Quarterly, 14*(4), 317–326.

Müller-Brockman, J. (1996). *Grid Systems in Graphic Design/Raster Systeme für die visuelle Gestaltung.* Salenstein, Switzerland: Niggli.

Nanyang Technical University Libraries. (2017, Mar. 22). Origins and evolution of writing systems. https://blogs.ntu.edu.sg/hss-language-evolution/wiki/chapter-17

Polgar, D. R. (2017, August 4). Don't just learn to code: Silicon Valley needs more fuzzies. BigThink. Retrieved from https://bigthink.com/david-ryan-polgar/dont-just -learn-to-code-silicon-valley-needs-more-fuzzy-thinkers

Tschichold, J. (1928). *Die neue Typographie: Ein Handbuch für zeitgemäss schaffende.* Berlin: Verlag des Bildungsverbandes der deutschen Buchdrucker.

Zhao, S., & Baldauf, R. B. (2008). *Planning Chinese characters: Reaction, evolution or revolution?* Dordrecht: Springer.

## CHAPTER 4

The Technology of Information Visualization

To understand how visualization applications get the data for the visualization, we review how data are gathered, structured in ways that can be shared and parsed for visualizations, and prepared for further analysis.

PREPARING TO CREATE YOUR OWN VISUALIZATIONS

In this section we begin to combine the concepts of turning data into information, and reflect on the principles of layout, message construction and interpretation, and the building blocks of any graphic and visualization—the "visual semantics" of visual communication.

The transition from concept to computing is a bridge created by applying basic web tools and interactivity. There are many online and in-class tutorials about these tools, specifically HTML, cascading style sheets, and JavaScript. These are our starting points. The first chapters of Scott Murray's *Interactive Information Visualization for the Web* (review of HTML, CSS, and JS), Mozilla Developers' Network (MDN, a more thorough training tool: https://developer.mozilla.org/en-US/), and w3schools (a broader tech-skills site that includes HTML, CSS, JavaScript, PHP, mySQL, XML, and json tutorials: https://www.w3schools.com/), among many others, are recommended. Each of these addresses similar content with different examples and different teaching approaches. Take a look and see which online text "speaks to you."

There are two keys to understanding how to integrate data, web pages, graphics, and interactivity. The first is that HTML, XML, and their instantiations, such as scalable vector graphics (SVG), are implementations of Standard Generalized Markup Language (SGML, https://www.w3.org/MarkUp/SGML/) and together represent the *structure* of the data and separately the *content of the data* in a hierarchical tree. The second key is the DOM—the document object model—a hierarchical representation of the tags that we manipulate using JavaScript and d3. The hierarchy starts with a "root tag," then branching into nodes and leaves, creating parent-child relationships (figure 4.1).

We get a closer look at how this tree is realized when viewing an XML page. As HTML and XML share the same structural rules, web browsers can read any HTML or XML file. However, the browser is preprogrammed with a "document type definition" or commands that interpret the .html tags. The <strong> tag, for instance, changes the *presentation of the data content* of a given tag to be *displayed* in a bold font. We gain greater control over the visual display of our data by applying a cascading style sheet (CSS). There is no inherent association between the command to bold (e.g., <b> or <strong>) and the *content* being emboldened. For instance, which tag better indicates the data for the concept of an "author": <author>Shakespeare</author>, or <strong>Shakespeare</strong>?

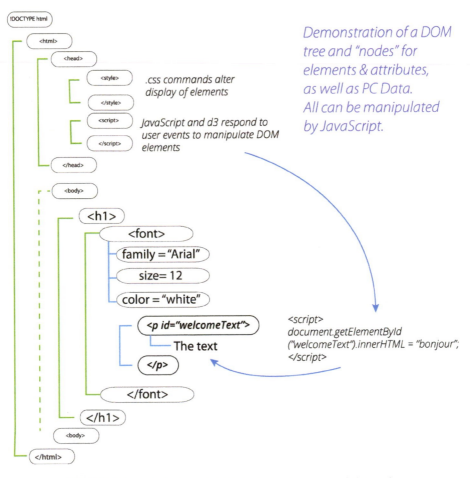

FIGURE 4.1 A DOM tree with HTML tags. *Courtesy of the author*

XML files do not contain commands controlling the display of the data, so a browser will display what it can interpret, which is just the hierarchical tree.

```
<?xml version="1.0"?>
<books>
    <book id="RK777">
        <author>Hunt, Rita</author>
        <title>Field Guide to New England Birds</title>
        <genre>Outdoor activities</genre>
        <price>44.95</price>
        <publish_date>2018-01-13</publish_date>
        <description>An in-depth review of where and how to locate songbirds of the North East.
        </description>
    </book>
    <book id="OL1700">
        <author>O'Brien, Patrick</author>
        <title>Master and Commander</title>
        <genre>Adventure</genre>
        <genre>Nautical</genre>
        <price>25.95</price>
        <publish_date>1991-06-06</publish_date>
        <description>First in the 21 volume series of John Aubrey, RN, and his friend Dr. Steven
            Maturin during the Napoleonic wars.
        </description>
    </book>
    <book id="DC3999">
        <author>Crabill, David</author>
        <title>Management Techniques</title>
        <genre>Fantasy</genre>
        <price>18.95</price>
        <publish_date>2018-11-23</publish_date>
        <description>Part of the Harvard Business School small publications for administrators
            this groundbreaking work guides upper management to more effective and efficient
            work.</description>
    </book>
    <book id="RV2099">
        <author>Vanderweit, Ryan</author>
        <title>Two Tours</title>
        <genre>Military</genre>
        <price>18.95</price>
        <publish_date>2018-09-08</publish_date>
        <description>The true story of an infantryman serving two terms in Iraq and
            Afghanistan.</description>
    </book>
</books>
```

Different browsers (Safari, Internet Explorer, Opera, Firefox, Aloha, and so on) display the hierarchical tree differently, the output varying both by the type of browser and the release version of that browser. The Safari browser shows the content between tags, but none of the tagging; other browsers display a hierarchical tree of the tags and content, with a warning message that there is no style sheet data associated with the source XML file (figure 4.2).

This XML file does not appear to have any style information associated with it. The document tree is shown below.

```
▼<catalog>
  ▼<book id="RK777">
      <author>Hunt, Rita</author>
      <title>Field Guide to New England Birds</title>
      <genre>Outdoor activities</genre>
      <price>44.95</price>
      <publish_date>2018-01-13</publish_date>
    ▼<description>
        An in-depth review of where and how to locate songbirds of the North East.
      </description>
    </book>
  ▼<book id="OL1700">
      <author>O'Brien, Patrick</author>
      <title>Master and Commander</title>
      <genre>Adventure</genre>
      <price>25.95</price>
      <publish_date>1991-06-06</publish_date>
    ▼<description>
        First in the 21 volume series of John Aubrey, RN, and his friend Dr. Steven Maturin durir
      </description>
    </book>
  ▼<book id="DC3999">
      <author>Crabill, David</author>
      <title>Management Techniques</title>
      <genre>Fantasy</genre>
      <price>18.95</price>
      <publish_date>2018-11-23</publish_date>
    ▼<description>
        Part of the Harvard Business School small publications for administrators this groundbre:
        effective and efficient work.
      </description>
    </book>
  ▼<book id="RV2099">
      <author>Vanderweit, Ryan</author>
      <title>Two Tours</title>
      <genre>Military</genre>
      <price>18.95</price>
      <publish_date>2018-09-08</publish_date>
    ▼<description>
        The true story of an infantryman serving two terms in Iraq and Afghanistan.
      </description>
    </book>
  </catalog>
```

FIGURE 4.2 Output of an .xml file in Firefox. *Courtesy of the author*

Just as the *display possibilities* of data in an .html file are tailorable when applying CSS commands, so an XML file is supported by linking an XSL (extended stylesheet language and transformation) file. An XSL file combines features of a cascading style sheet with scriptlike ability to select and to transform some of the data in the browser. If there is an associated XSL file, the way a CSS file might be associated with an HTML file, then we could simultaneously select certain records (such as book id="RK777") and display an image of that book.

In the realm of information visualization, SVG is the favored way to express data for drawing. *Scaleable* means the graphic maintains the same size regardless of output device and size. Being an XML implementation, we can manipulate the nodes used to draw as we manipulate the nodes showing data in an HTML page. Just as we have <xml> tags for content, so we have <svg> for visual content.

SVG files can be created using a drawing tool such as Adobe Illustrator or the open source GIMP software, or by writing our own from scratch. SVG files maintain image clarity and color regardless of the output size and display device because the image is not a group of pixels to make an image, but essentially a formula that draws the shapes according to x, y coordinates and curve arcs and line angles. SVG commands are drawn in the browser without any other special instructions such as XSL, although it is common to apply CSS commands.

In the following example, some basic shapes (our "visual primitives") are demonstrated: circle, line, a polygon, and a square. Notice the <svg> tag defines the container for drawing the object. The circle example creates a drawing panel of 100 pixels by 100 pixels. In that panel a circle is drawn at the x, y location *in the panel*, starting in the middle ($x = 50$, $y = 50$). Finally the circle is drawn with a radius of 40 pixels, then filled with the color red with a black outline, using an inline CSS command.

Circle:
```
<svg height="100" width="100">
    <circle cx="50" cy="50" r="40" stroke="black" stroke-width="3" fill="red" />
</svg>
```

Line:
```
<svg height="210" width="500">
    <line x1="0" y1="0" x2="200" y2="200" style="stroke:rgba(255,0,0,0.5);stroke-width:2" />
</svg>
```

Polygon:
```
<svg height="250" width="500">
    polygon points="220,10 300,210 170,250 123,234"
    style="fill:pink;stroke:purple;stroke-width:1" />
</svg>
```

Rectangle (square):
```
<svg width="400" height="180">
    <rect x="50" y="20" width="150" height="150"
    style="fill:blue;stroke:pink;stroke-width:5;fill-opacity:0.1;stroke-opacity:0.9" />
</svg>
```

Data to be visualized could be stored on your local computer or distributed through networked systems, such as web servers, databases, and file servers.

Generally in InfoVis, the data and the display of the data are two separate functions. Data are stored in various file formats, such as in a relational database, flat files (aka text files), .json (JavaScript object notation) and .xml files, and so on. Data in these files are usually retrieved from a server, and there are several technologies and techniques to achieve this, depending on the file types. Typically the data from a server may be (a) streamed back to a browser and displayed (just as web pages are), or (b) stored on the server in a file or files; the data and display information are combined in real time by a program or script running on the server. For example, say we want to retrieve data from a rare book collection stored in a relational database management system (RDBMS). The end user submits a query in his browser; the <action> tag sends the request to the server; in turn, software on the server processes the request, queries the database, and creates a list of matches. These raw data need to be integrated with HTML and CSS commands to display them correctly back on the user's browser. This technique results in a "stateless" data; that means the data are not saved to disk to be recalled at will, but the results are lost when the user ends the session.

The results of that query could also be saved to a file—in any of the formats mentioned above. Ultimately a very large collection of data, metadata, user transaction log records, and more, are created. To explain this better, we look at a common system architecture, such as the Internet, as a "client-server model." The variety of data, volume of data, and their variability are prime reasons why visualization is useful in understanding the data and are the rationale behind big data, business intelligence, and visual analytics.

Client-Server Architecture: How to Get Data Presented

Figure 4.3 demonstrates the path that a request for data can take, and some of the helper technologies creating the final display to the user.

The steps involved in sending an end user's "request" (an HTTP Request Object) and receiving a "response" (HTTP Response Object) from the server are as follows (see https://www.w3schools.com/xml/dom_http.asp for more):

- A query is submitted by the end user through a browser <form> to the server.
- The server receives the query and a script or program is called. The query is passed to that program (the script/program in the "action=" statement of the <form>, e.g., <form method="post" action="getMyData.php">).
- The program converts the query into an SQL statement and then communicates with a relational database server to run the query. The retrieved data are called a result set. (The particulars of the result set need not detain us here.)

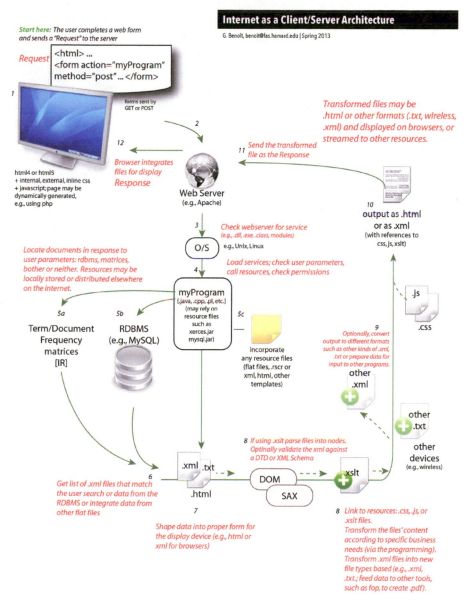

Start here: *The user completes a web form and sends a "Request" to the server*

Request

```
<html> ...
<form action="myProgram"
method="post" ... </form>
```

1

forms sent by
GET or POST

2

html4 or html5
+ internal, external, inline css
+ javascript; page may be
dynamically generated,
e.g., using php

*Browser integrates
files for display*

Response

12

11 *Send the transformed
file as the Response*

Web Server
(e.g., Apache)

*Transformed files may be
.html or other formats (.txt, wireless,
.xml) and displayed on browsers, or
streamed to other resources.*

10

**output as .html
or as .xml**
(with references to
css, js, xslt)

3

O/S   e.g., Unix, Linux

Check webserver for service
(e.g., .dll, .exe, .class, modules)

*Locate documents in response to
user parameters: rdbms, matrices,
bother or neither. Resources may be
locally stored or distributed elsewhere
on the internet.*

4

*Load services; check user parameters,
call resources, check permissions*

myProgram
[.java, .cpp, .pl, etc.]
(may rely on
resource files
such as
xerces.jar
mysql.jar)

5a

**Term/Document
Frequency
matrices
[IR]**

5b

RDBMS
(e.g., MySQL)

5c

incorporate
any resource files
(flat files, .rscr or
xml, html, other
templates)

.js

.css

9
*Optionally, convert
output to different formats
such as other kinds of .xml,
.txt or prepare data for
input to other programs.*

other
.xml

other
.txt

other
devices
(e.g., wireless)

6
*Get list of .xml files that match
the user search or data from the
RDBMS or integrate data from
other flat files*

.xml .txt

.html

7
*Shape data into proper form for
the display device (e.g., html or
xml for browsers)*

8 *If using .xslt parse files into nodes.
Optionally validate the xml against
a DTD or XML Schema*

DOM

SAX

xslt

8 *Link to resources: .css, .js, or
.xslt files.
Transform the files' content
according to specific business
needs (via the programming).
Transform .xml files into new
file types based (e.g., .xml,
.txt.; feed data to other tools,
such as fop, to create .pdf).*

FIGURE 4.3 The client-server architecture showing the path from the user's web form through the server, gathering data from several resources, and adding other files (such as .css) and finally returning the data to the end user. *Courtesy of the author*

- Alternatively, the user's query is processed and may be passed to a program that does not use RDBMS but rather other file types (e.g., .tsv, .csv, .json, .xml, .txt). In the realm of big data, there are specialized software applications and server architectures, called "information ecologies," such as Snowflake (https://www.snowflake.net/about/), Apache Hadoop (http://hadoop.apache.org), or Apache Spark (https://spark.apache.org), that use the cloud for storage and other database techniques, such as MongoDB or the Apache Distributed File System (HDFS: https://hadoop.apache.org/docs/r1.2.1/hdfs_design.html).
- The data in the result set may not be consistent, or may have missing values. Imagine a file that contains the research subjects' name, age, and gender. The age field could hold data that are not possible (such as negative number), or not likely (someone accidentally enters "120" instead "20"), or missing. In these cases, the data have to be "cleaned" of these problems. Files that have been cleaned are collected to create a "data warehouse" (Benoît, 2005). (This is described in detail in appendix A).
- One technique is to map fields from one dataset to the fields of another dataset, and then process the heterogeneous data through any number of crosswalks.
- The server-side program could equally integrate the heterogeneous data and output the results in a file structure that is less sensitive to missing values, or a structure in which the data can be tested. Some of these output files include .xml, .json, and tab-delimited, among others.
- Finally, the prepared data results may be
  - integrated with structure tags to enable the browser to display the data, usually integrating CSS for *presentation* and JavaScript for *interactivity*; or
  - streamed to other commercial software and big data systems.

In this framework, the data can be shaped to integrate HTML with drawing commands in SVG as well as incorporating a JavaScript library, d3.js, that creates an information graphic in the browser. To advance to InfoVis, we need to support end user interactivity.

INTERACTIVITY

Browsers allow the end user to communicate with the computer through a variety of "events." Stated differently, interaction with a browser using JavaScript "registers" different event handlers on elements in the DOM tree. Table 4.1 is a list of events, followed by use examples.

Mouse:	onclick	Clipboard:	oncopy	Animation:
	oncontextmenu		oncut	
	ondblclick		onpaste	
	onmousedown			Transition:
	onmouseenter	Print:	onafterprint	
	onmouseleave		onbeforeprint	
	onmousemove			Server-Sent:
	onmouseover	Media:	onabort	
	onmouseout		oncanplay	
	onmouseup		oncanplaythrough	Misc:
Keyboard:	onkeydown		ondurationchange	
	onkeypress		onemptied	
	onkeyup		onended	
			onerror	
Frame/Object:	onabort		onloadedmetadata	
	onbeforeunload		onloadstart	
	onerror		onpause	
	onhashchange		onpause	Touch:
	onload		onplay	
	onpageshow		onplaying	
	onpagehide		onprogress	
	onresize		onratechange	In addition to these specific events, there are "objects" whose contents we can poll, such as whether an event is "trusted," whether the control key is being pressed, and how much a mouse wheel is moved.
	onscroll		onseeked	
	onunload		onseeking	
Form:	onblur		onstalled	
	onchange		onsuspend	
	onfocus		ontimeupdate	
	onfocusin		onvolumechange	
	onfocusout		onwaiting	
	oninput			
	oninvalid			
	onreset		The complete list is at https://www.w3schools.com/jsref/dom_obj_event.asp	
	onsearch			
	onselect			
	onsubmit			
Drag:	ondrag			
	ondragend			
	ondragenter			
	ondragleave			
	ondragover			
	ondragstart			
	ondrop			

For example, "onclick" is one of the first mouse events we see. When the end user clicks the mouse, a mouse event is generated. The "events" are calls from the end user to the operating system and application to respond to the input. Clicking on some area of the web page has been scripted to respond to the onclick. In this JavaScript example, clicking on some text in the browser causes the text in the <p> tag to change:

<p> id="test" onclick="changeText()">Greetings</p>.

Substitute other events for the onclick to provide a surprisingly full range of communication between the end user and the computer, through the visualization.

This example from d3 shows the addition of the equivalent onclick. The .on() adds mouse-listening capabilities to a visual object drawn by d3. While the JavaScript calls a function named "changeText()", the d3 version uses an anonymous function. The result is the same: upon clicking the mouse, a function is called to perform some work. The JavaScript events above have equivalents in d3; for example, .on("mouseover" . . .).

```
var rows = svg.selectAll('rect' + ' .row-' + (n + 1))
        .data(d3.range(squaresRow))
        .enter().append('rect')
        .on("click", function() {
```

The .data is a d3 command to identify the actual source data and which loads the data into memory. Here we ask d3 to determine the range (values) of the data. The enter() function acts as if we, the user, pressed the "enter" key to load the data. Upon entering the data, we append a rectangle ("rect") to the svg object. Finally, let's add the ability to "listen" to the mouse clicks. The "on" triggers the rectangle to "listen" to the click; The "click" is one of the many actions we can listen to - equivalent to JavaScript's ... onclick=myFunction();

```
        var coords=d3.mouse(this);

        alert("hit coords "+coords);
```

Capture the screen's x,y coordinates of the click (in pixels).
Use JavaScript's own alert() function and pass the mouse coordinates captured by d3.

Communication with a Computer? The Progression from Data to Information

By combining these types of events that act as communication requests from the end user, we can cause our visual display to respond, also as a communicator. A slightly controversial perspective that considers human-computer action using a visual language (the semantics) and thoughtful composition of layout, type, color, position, and inference (visual syntax), we can cast the limited use of interactive opportunities as a "conversation" between the data and the person viewing and interacting with those data. This is the critical point in information visualization.

Some researchers hold that people project interpretations onto a painting or other visual; is there really much difference between a painting or a digital image? Be it a painting or a digital image, "seeing comes before words," and there is an "always-present gap between words and seeing" that cause or allow us to engage in an inner dialogue (Berger, 1972).

I believe that a user experience (UX) event is no different from any other communicative event. The participants start in one state of affairs and progress until some conclusion—either there is no successfully shared goal or, ideally, there is some sharable goal to establish meaning. From that start state, the viewer/speaker has a question—"how to do this task?" or "what is important here?" We could argue that this is the impetus for the *query*. The *response* from the computer is the reply, a proposition: it is a potentially useful, interpretable reply, warranting consideration by the recipient. That, in turn, should spark engagement or kind of back-and-forth conversation with the user. The engagement could be rather elementary, such as just reading the answer online. Or it may prompt other questions in the person's mind, such as the need for more details, or exploring some contradiction. In human-human communication, these thoughts are expressed as "secondary streams of discourse" where both parties remain on the main point, but are free to ask related questions in conversations that clarify details or intentionality. For instance, consider this exchange:

A: "I just fed the dog . . . "
B: "A dog?! I thought you had a cat."
A: "Oh, yes, of course, just a slip of the tongue . . ." and the primary conversation continues. (This is well-documented in communication studies and is an example of a "language game.")

In the same way, an interactive information visualization is a sustainable "discourse" paralleling discourse between an end user and an online game. As either the player causes the graphics to respond, or the game's programming causes the graphics to progress, the change causes a response or a change in state, and either side takes a further action. The game may be programmed to a large but limited number of responses, and the human player sees and internalizes them in order to make sense of the change. With understanding comes the motivation to take a likely successful next action, as well as understanding of *why* to take the next action. This means the person has constructed something meaningful in his or her mind and, if asked, could explain the rationale for this decision. It evinces, too, the concept of trust in a decision that it is trustworthy and believable, as mentioned in the chapter on aesthetics. With the exception of a strategy of game-playing in which deceit is an allowable action, there is the underlying sense of the truthfulness of the meaning and justifiable action. The Media Studies' (2007) concept of "co-construction of meaning" applies here.

Hands-On Practice

We now move to practicing d3 to create basic images and integrate basic interactivity. The goal is to become comfortable with the structure of d3 as we progress rather rapidly toward creating interactive visualizations. For these exercises, consider using Firefox, Chrome, or Safari, and viewing the data using the console window.

Following Kandinsky, Bertin (1967, 1977) and Keim (2002) state that there are repertories of the semantics we have to work with (see table 4.2).

HANDS-ON LAB 1 (JAVASCRIPT AND D3.JS)

Note: Most chapters have additional readings/notes and hands-on labs posted on the companion website.

Creating your own interactive information visualizations can be challenging, but by combining knowledge of graphic design, aesthetics, scripting, and HTML, you can own your own visualizations. This way you understand and guide the viewers' understanding and exploration of the data.

In this how-to guide, we'll use certain examples that may not represent the entirety of the standards, but are focused to important aspects we need for this tutorial.

A web browser displays *static* data from a web page. Adding CSS changes the display of the data. Adding JavaScript allows interactivity with the end user, and dynamism to the webpage. Adding other JavaScript libraries, specifically the d3.js library, allows us to manipulate the HTML page (through its DOM tree), by (a) static data already hard-coded on our web page, or (b) by pulling data from a web server. The d3.js library has built-in functions to read data that are stored on our web page as well as load data into memory (RAM) by reading comma-separated value files (.csv), tab-delimited files (.tsv), .xml files, and .json files. We can visualize data as a snapshot of a period of time, or we can receive updates to our data in milliseconds.

Tech Hands-On

For the hands-on component, we suggest practicing with d3 to learn the mechanics and thought processes of designing a useful visualization. Later, experiment with commercial applications such as Tableau, using its free demo/learning application to experience the differences between a data-focused application and being responsible for an entire visualization experience.

	TABLE 4.2	
Elements	**What is conveyed**	**How (graphically) to convey in a design (aesthetics)**
Line	• straight suggest distance • curved lines • vertical lines suggest height, strength of association • jagged lines suggest lack of pattern	• freehand (personal, casual) • mechanical (feeling of being based on data) • continuous lines (especially with arrows): directs the viewers' eye movement • broken lines: suggests ephemeral or insubstantial • line thickness: suggests strength of association • thin lines: suggest weak association or interpretative frames (such as units of measurement, or "ticks")
Shape	squares, rectangles circles, ellipses triangles	• squares and circles represent an identifiable unit, generally distinct from each other: the "visual primitives" • circles suggest continuous movement, and often overlap to suggest shared properties and/or to identify a cluster of related items (such as squares and other circles)
Tone	contrast illusion of form sense of "feeling" of the image depth and distance rhythm and patterns	• helps set the aesthetic mood: technical, modern art, futuristic, old-fashioned feeling, etc. • a sense of unfolding in storytelling • visually suggestive (generative metaphor)
Color	light/tone patterns forms symbols suggests movement suggests patterns (harmonic) contrasts mood	• use of color as light and contrasts helps identify major clusters of related data and minor clusters of related data in a larger visual unit • symbols can help the eye distinguish the main part of the intended message as well as identify the unusual ("interesting") events in the data that lead to new knowledge • can suggest movement, particularly to time series • help to set the tone or mood of the visual to attract and hold the viewer's eye
Pattern	patterns: natural or man-made	Natural patterns such as Fibonacci numbers or seashells as the basis for the Golden Mean; man-made patterns suggest both realistic images (such as a human face) or patterns that suggest something either recognizable (such as a face) or something novel that needs investigation.
Texture	optical, physical, ephemeral	Optical texture creates the illusion of texture; perhaps how we might express layering in visualization. Physical is where the design (see lines) suggests subtle, perhaps unexpected details in the data. Ephemeral textures are mutable, either by the end user's interactions or by a script changing the data in the visualization,
Form	representational or abstract	In visualization we might think of this as the choice between creating 3d or 2d images.
Adapted from http://www.artyfactory.com/art_appreciation/visual-elements/visual-elements.html		

It is strongly recommended that you take advantage of the online training Tableau offers at https://www.tableau.com/learn/training.

d3.js is a very popular library for creating visualizations displayed in the browser. To use d3, you must be comfortable using

- A text editor (Atom, TextWrangler, NotePad++, others)
- HTML (version 5)
- CSS—both inline, internal, and external files
- JavaScript fundamentals (such as declaring variables, functions)

It is useful, but not required, to have some experience with jQuery and SVG.

HTML supports several ways to display graphics and support interactivity. HTML5 supports drawing in an object, called a canvas, and by applying scalable vector graphics. We focus here only on SVG.

We can draw objects with SVG without using any helper libraries, such as d3.js, or we can design images using Adobe Illustrator and saving the file as an .svg and then pasting the .svg file in your HTML page. Check the w3schools' introduction to SVG (https://www.w3schools.com/graphics/svg_intro.asp) or the more complete Mozilla Developers' Network (MDN web docs: https://developer.mozilla.org/en-US/docs/Web/SVG). Maps play a significant role in InfoVis, so it is useful to examine other libraries, such as jVectorMap (http://jvectormap.com/) and some of the power of SVG (http://svg-wow.org).

HTML: Building from the Basics

A web page typically has a header area, content area, and a footer area that end users can see; there are also areas in the web page just for the browser to see.

```
<!DOCTYPE html>
<html>
    <head>
        <title>
        <meta charset="utf-8"/>
            // javascript functions appear here
        </script>
        <style>
            p { font-family: "Avenir Next" sans-serif;
                color: cornflowerblue;
            }
        </style>
    </head>

    <body>
        <header>This is an html header area</header>
        This is the main content area
        <footer>This is a footer.</footer>
    </body>

</html>
```

Notes: Tags between the <!DOCTYPE and the </head> tag are not displayed to the user. This area holds commands about how to display the data in the css area; and those for dynamic responses, such as changing the display (via various events, e.g., "mouse events").

In the body area we have the main content. The content can be updated dynamically by getting new data from a server.

CSS

CSS allows us to change the *visual* display of the data by (a) changing the display commands of HTML tags, or by (b) a group of elements (called a class), or by (c) changing the tag (or element) by its ID number. For example, to change all the text in a paragraph tag (<p> tag), overwrite the default behavior of the <p> tag with your own commands, for example:

```
p {
    font-family: "Avenir Next" sans serif; color: cornflowerblue;
}
```

To change a *unique* element identified by an ID, for example, a paragraph called infotext:

```
#infotext {
    font-size: 12px;
}
```

In the body of the HTML, we could apply this tag: <p id="infotext">Greetings, folks.</p>. There can be only one element with an ID in a webpage.

A group of functionally similar content can be altered all at once by classing them together (for example, <p class="details">These are details.</p>):

```
.details {
    color: red;
}
```

Say we want the title and other details on our site to be red:

```
<h1 class="details">
Visualizing Solutions
</h1>
<p>This text will appear without any specific visual commands.</p>
<div class="details">And here are some details!</div>
```

DOM

The tags, classes, IDs, and scripts come together in the computing object, the Document Object Model (DOM). Because the DOM is a hierarchy, the browser interprets the tags as a parent-child relationship. In addition, the DOM tree builds in the computer's memory a reference to all the properties of the tag. The <p> tag has hidden properties describing the font family, font size, color, line height, and more. We can change these hidden visual behaviors by interacting with the DOM tree using our scripts.

Every tree has a *single root element*. The elements are the tags; tags have properties or attributes to provide more detail about the element, such as ID, name, class, and color. An HTML page's tags (elements) are the branches of this tree:

<!DOCTYPE html	*Document type definition (dtd) for html5*
<html>	*Root*
<head>	This area controls the rest of the display.
<meta> </meta>	Meta tags are useful for SEO, charsets.
<style> </style>	
<script> </style>	
<body>	Tags in <body> appear in the browser.
<header>	
content	
<footer>	
</body>	The closing tag for <body>
</html>	Close the HTML!

Using JavaScript, we can change dynamically the elements in the DOM tree by accessing them and then issuing a new command. For example, we can select an HTML document element by its ID and change what the text says. In the body of a page, say we have the following:

```
<p id="test" onclick="changeText()">Greetings</p>
```

Later in the webpage, we can change the contents ("Greetings") by clicking on the text. Clicking on the text calls a JavaScript function we can write, here called changeText(). The changeText() function is in the <script> area.

```
<script>
    function changeText() {
        document.getElementById("test").innerHTML = "Bonjour";
    }
</script>
```

JavaScript can access the DOM tree of a web page, allowing us to change the page as we wish. We can also calculate data and display the new data. Here we change the text of our "test" element by performing some arithmetic and sending the results back to our test element:

```
<script>
    function changeText() {
        var x = 20;
        var y = 4;
        var results = x * y;
        document.getElementById("test").innerHTML = "The results are " + results;
    }
</script>
```

SVG

SVG is a way of drawing images by providing the coordinates, color, height, width, and other properties as "attributes" to the predefined "elements" of SVG: among them rect (for squares and rectangles), circle (for circles and ovals), ellipse, line, polyline, polygon, and path. The benefit of using SVG is that we can store both the data and the commands to draw images based on the data. Here we have a <rect> element with several attributes:

```
<svg width="400" height="100">

 <rect width="300" height="100"
    style="fill:red);stroke-width:3;
    stroke:rgb(0,0,0)"/>


</svg>
```

Define the dimensions of the svg container that will hold the image: width and height.
Define the dimensions of the SVG object (here <rect>).
And add inline CSS commands to assign a color: fill: rgb(red) and an outline (of 3 pixels) in black (rgb(0,0,0)):
Close the svg element

Here is an example of an SVG file embedded in an HTML file:

```
<!DOCTYPE html>
<html>
    <body>
        <svg height="100" width="100">
            <circle cx="50" cy="50" r="40" stroke="orange"
            stroke-width="3"
            fill="olive" />
            Sorry, your browser does not support inline SVG.
        </svg>
    </body>
</html>
```

Let's review a moment. The <svg> node is one that is built into JavaScript. The drawing area of the SVG is defined by the height and width elements. This important. On the second line, a <circle> is defined on a grid. The *x*-axis on your computer screen starts in the upper left of the screen and extends to the right edge in a straight line. The *y*-axis also starts in the upper left and extends vertically downward. The top left corner is represented as (0,0). The cx and cy of our circle means the "center of the circle is at (50,50)" (50 pixels to the right and then 50 pixels down vertically.) The radius is defined with r (and here is 40 pixels wide). Finally we can identify the foreground of the image—a black circle, with a border three pixels wide, filled in red. If the browser cannot support SVG, then an error message ("Sorry . . .") is displayed. We close the SVG as we do all elements, with a closing tag </svg>.

HTML, SVG, XML, and others are all implementations of Standard Generalized Markup Language (SGML). The key to their interoperability and our ability to manipulate the files is the DOM that structures the data in the file as a hierarchical tree, starting with a root and then nodes and leaves.

Integrating the d3 Library

The d3 library lets us define a graphic object and then attach elements and attributes, as well as JavaScript. A typical technique is to define the graphic object as SVG. Note that these two SVGs are not the same thing. Read this example from Scott Murray's online text (chapter 5, example 08):

```
1   <!DOCTYPE html>
2   <html lang="en">
3       <head>
4           <meta charset="utf-8">
5           <title>D3: Setting paragraphs' style conditionally, based on data
6           </title>
7           <script src="../d3.js"></script>
8       </head>
9   <body>
10      <script type="text/javascript">
11          var dataset = [ 5, 10, 15, 20, 25 ];
12          d3.select("body").selectAll("p")
13              .data(dataset)
14              .enter()
15              .append("p")
16              .text(function(d) {
17                  return "I can count up to " + d;
18              })
19              .style("color", function(d) {
20                  if (d > 15) {   //Threshold of 15
21                      return "red";
22                  } else {
23                      return "black";
24                  }
25              });
26
27      </script>
28  </body>
29  </html>
```

Line 7 links the d3 library to our page.

Line 11 is an array of data; the variable name is "dataset." Each element (5, 10 . . . 25) will be processed one by one; the value of d on the first pass is 5 and the value of i is 0.

Line 12 is d3.select("body").selectAll("p"). The d3 here refers to the d3 object defined in the d3.js library. Now we "select" the <body> tag in the HTML page and attach it to the d3 object we just defined. The selectAll("p") means to "select all the <p> tags that belong to the <body> element" so that we can add, delete, and otherwise manipulate the attributes of the <p> tag. Also we can add new <p> tags to the DOM tree.

```
15      .data(dataset)
16      .enter()
17      .append("p")
18      .text(function(d) {
19          return "I can count up to " + d;
20      })
```

Line 15, .data(dataset), loads the data from the array dataset. This is not unlike typing in the data by hand. The data from the dataset array are loaded in the computer memory to be used by the script. Instead of writing a loop to read the data, the .data() function automatically loops through all the data and stores these in memory via the .enter() function. Once we have data in memory, we can add other HTML tags. Usually we write our own functions, but d3 allows "creating a function on the fly"—hence, anonymous.

Lines 18 to 20 demonstrate an anonymous function. d3 has two default variables— "d" for datum, and "i" for iterator. The .text appends the text to be shown in the <p> </p> block. This is the same as saying the JavaScript command

```
document.getElementByTag("p").innerHTML = "I can count up to";
```

The anonymous function has no name (hence, just "function"). This example accepts a parameter (the d, here meaning the variable d, which stands for datum) and returns a string of data ("I can count up to 5") and then automatically appends this string to the new p, using the .text() method.

Lines 21 to 27 demonstrate two great features of d3. First notice we can define cascading stylesheet commands to the newly created <p>. This is the same as

```
document.getElementByTag("p").style.color = "red";
```

```
21              .style("color", function(d) {
22                  if (d > 15) {    //Threshold of 15
23                      return "red";
24                  } else {
25                      return "black";
26                  }
27              });
```

Where does the "d" come from? It is built into d3 and instantiated automatically.

var dataset = [5, 10, 15, 20, 25];

The array "dataset" has five values. Line 22 is an "if" statement that says if the value of the variable d is greater than 15, then return the color red, meaning return the string that says the same as the JavaScript command style.color = "red". Otherwise return style.color = "black".

The complete set of commands (or methods) for d3 are available from GitHub (https://github.com/d3/d3/blob/master/API.md). Check the wiki (https://github .com/d3/d3/wiki) for directions about running d3.js locally. The latest browsers do not support a mix-and-match approach of http:// and https://. If you have your own web server software on your computer, or can use one at work or school, it is worth testing your scripts on the server to prevent this error. The Macintosh computers have a built-in web server; for Windows, you can download the Apache web server (http://www.apache.org).

The d3 library and examples are covered by the Open Source Initiative Public License, version 3 (figure 4.4) (https://opensource.org/licenses/GPL-3.0). Please be sure to follow these when creating your own visualizations.

Link to the d3 library in the <script> section of the header of your web page. Note that there are different versions. d3 is a JavaScript library, and so we can

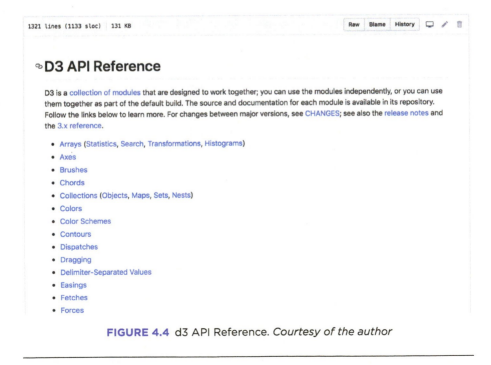

FIGURE 4.4 d3 API Reference. *Courtesy of the author*

alter the DOM tree of the web page by adding elements and providing data for the attributes. First, define an SVG container and then select an existing element (such as <body>) and add it. Once the SVG container is added, we can add more elements and attributes to the graphic elements (rect, circle, etc.). (We can label the container anything we want, so let's call it "container.") We can issue a JavaScript command all on one line or, for the sake of legibility, break it up at the dot.

Drawing a box with d3 combines both commands from the d3 library (and the main object called "d3") and then integrates HTML and SVG elements.

```
<script>
    var container = d3.select("body").append("svg")
        .attr("width", 400)
        .attr("height", 400)
        .style("border", "1px solid gray");

    // now draw a rect in the container:
    var myrectangle = container.append("rect")
        attr("x", 10)
        .attr("y", 10)
        .attr("width", 50)
        .attr("height", 50);
</script>
```

For demo, the container will have a gray line around it so we can see its area - this is where all drawing must be appear

Be sure to remember we declare a variable first ...

Here are other items to draw. Here's a circle that is situated at the 50,50 point in the container with a radius of 25 pixels.

```
var container = d3.select("body").append("svg")
    .attr("width", 300)
    .attr("height", 300);
// draw a circle
var mycircle = container.append("circle")
    .attr("cx", 50)
    .attr("cy", 50)
    .attr("r", 25);
```

Remember - we need a container (call it what you want) in which d3 can draw. To use this container, it must be bound to some HTML tag. Usually "body" but it doesn't have to be. Then we have to add a way to draw. That is the addition of a drawing area - here it is called svg. It doesn't have to be - it's just a convention. Line-by-line the additional lines (those starting with the . dot are applied or affect the variable defined above them Finally, we add some d3 item to the container.

Here's a line:

```
var container = d3.select("body").append("svg")
    .attr("width", 200)
    .attr("height", 200);
// now a line starting from x, y to another x,y position:
var myline = container.append("line")
    .attr("x1", 5)
    .attr("y1", 5)
    .attr("x2",100)
    .attr("x3",100)
    .attr("stroke-width", 1)
    .attr("stroke", "red");
```

For polygons, we need a set of *x, y* coordinates to define a shape and, like the above commands, to add attributes such as color, line width (stroke), and fill color.

THE DATA FOR DISPLAY—BINDING

So far, the data needed for drawing the graphics have been hard-coded in our scripts. It's more useful to have the data also in a JavaScript variable (such as an array) and then draw them; and later we'll see it is still better to have the data in a different kind of container (such as in a data structure called .json). Notes are in crimson on the right side—don't type them.

```
var circlespaces = [100, 200, 300];
var container = d3.select("body").append("svg")

    .attr("width", 500)
    .attr("height", 500);

var circles = container.selectAll("circle")
    .data(circlespaces
    .enter()
    .append("circle");
var circleAttributes = circles.attr("cx",
    function(d)  return d; )
    .attr("cy", function (d)  return d; )
    .attr("r", 20)
    .style("fill", function(d)
        var colorToUse;
            if (d === 100) {
                colorToUse = "pink";
            } else if (d === 200)
                colorToUse = "yellow";
            } else if (d === 300)
                colorToUse = "red";
        });
```

Define the location of the circles
as before have d3 select the DOM body; add
container
Assign the width and height attributes of the container

The "selectAll" acts like a loop - read all the data in
the circlespaces *array one by one ...*
Load the data in memory - this "binds" the data
Create a circle
Rather than hard-code a value, this built-in function
uses its own parameter ("d" for datum) and returns
or assigned the result of the function ...

... here "d" is assigned a color (colorToUse) based
on the value of "d" - one by one each member of the
array is processed; the first time d is equal to
circlespaces[0], the first element in the array ... and
based on that value a color code is assigned (when d
is equal to 100, return the color "pink" and so on).

Better still, let's store the data in its own data structure. These data are still hard-coded, but they are separate from the commands for building the SVG elements. This means we can keep the code stable even when we change the values of the data. The values can come from our hard-coded .json structure, or we can read in data from a file, the same way we read in other JavaScript and CSS files. In real practice, we may read in data from a server—computer programs on the server preparing the data from other sources, and then saving them in the file we integrate. This is demonstrated below.

d3 has predefined functions that read several external resources, as well as being able to read data from a JavaScript array or a .json structure within the webpage/file.

- text file (e.g., .txt, .dat)
- .xml
- .html
- .csv (comma-separated value)
- .tsv (tab-separated value)
- .json
- XMLHttpRequest

Right now we want to "bind" the data from a .json file; a .json file holds a variable name and its value as a name-value pair. Strings must be in double quotes; integers do not.

```
var myCat = [{                          Define the object "myCat"
    "name": "Suky",                     Add some name/value pairs
    "age": "7",                         such as her "age" being "7"
    "favoriteActivity": "sleeping"
}];
```

We extract the data stored in the myCat variable by calling the variable name (myCat) and then asking for the property (or attribute) of the myCat that we want, for example, myCat.favoriteActivity returns "sleeping."

Above we tried a JavaScript array for the circles: var circlespaces = [100, 200, 300]. Now let's change the way we define the circles by placing all the data we need to define the location, size, and color attributes of the circle elements in a .json object. Once the data are defined, we'll "bind" the data to the objects for display.

```
var circlespaces = [                    Define the variable and grouped by square bracket [
    {                                   the first element starts with
        "theX": 100,
        "theY": 100,
        "theRadius": 50,
        "theColor": "pink"              and ends with
    },                                  separate individual items by the comma
    {
        "theX": 200,
        "theY": 200,
        "theRadius": 50,
        "theColor": "yellow"
    },
    {
        "theX": 300,
        "theY": 300,
        "theRadius": 50,
        "theColor": "red"
    }
];                                      The last ends the final element; the ] ends the group.
```

Just like the myCat example, now that we have stored data, we can access the data by calling the name of the object (circlespaces), the specific elements (which of the three circles we have defined), and the specific attributes of each element: for example,

circlespaces[0].theColor returns "pink"; circlespaces[1].theRadius returns 50; circlespaces[2].theY returns 300.

If you open the browser's console window, you'll see the data as the browser does:

__data__:

For the circlespaces, you'll see:

```
0: Array[3]
    <circle>
        __data__: Object
        theColor: "pink"
        theRadius: 50
        theY: 100
        theX: 100
```

Example 1

We want to draw a series of rectangles, color-coded so that we know which are related and how strongly they are related. In this example (figure 4.5), we create a series of rectangles, some text, and then respond to mouse-over, mouse-out, and onclick.

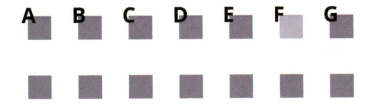

FIGURE 4.5 A sketch of a design for practicing d3. *Courtesy of the author*

Defining the dataset with .json might look like this:

```
var theRectangles = [
    {
        "x": 50,
        "y": 50,
        "theColor": "pink"
    }
]
```

Here's the full example with comments.

```
<!DOCTYPE html>
<html><head><title>Box Test</title>
<script src="d3.v4.min.js"></script>
<style>
    #infoBox {
        position: absolute;
        border-radius: 5px;
        background-color: olive;
        color: white;
        padding: 10px;
        font-size: 10px;
        text-align: center;
        top: 120px;
        left: 40%;
        z-index: 2;
    }
</style>
</head>
```

HTML5 declaration
Start of the <head> tag
Load the external d3.js file
CSS styles are defined. Here there is a single ID called "infoBox" defined. This box will be called later in the script. The script in the page will make this info box appear and show text when it is called. We will call this infoBox when the end-user clicks on a box.

There is a JavaScript that will hide and show the infoBox.

```
<body onload="hideBox()">
<div id="infoBox">This is the info box.</div>
<script>
    function hideBox() {
        document.getElementById("infoBox").style.display = "none";
    }
</script>
<script>
var w = 20;
var h = 20;
var startLine = 100;
var padding = 5;
var data = [1,2,3,4,5,6,7,8,9,10,11,12,13,14,15,16,17,18,19,20];
var textData = ["A","B","C","D","E","F","G","H","I","J",
    "K","L","M","N","O","P","Q","R","S","T","U"];

// create SVG element
var svg = d3.select("body")
    .append("svg")
    .style("border","1px solid silver")
    .attr("width", 800)
    .attr("height", 600);
```

When the page loads, a script is called to hide the infoBox. This line declares the infoBox and loads it on the page. Here we have the script that is called when the page loads and automatically hides ("display = 'none';).

Important: the "document.getElementById()" is how our script can access the HTML DOM tree elements. The script area is closed here - it doesn't have to be because we go right into another script ...

Getting ready: we declare and instantiate variables.

"data" is a JavaScript array we'll use for its "textData" is another array. If we used .json we could combine them into a more useful form.

Declare a variable (called "svg") and attach it to the body.

Optional: draw a line around the box so we can see it. The w x h of the drawing area. Our d3 commands will appear only in this area.

```
svg.selectAll("rect")
    .data(data)
    .enter()
    .append("rect")
    .attr("height", w)
    .attr("width",h)
    .attr("x", function(d, i)
        if (d <= 15) {
            return (i * 50) + 20;
        } else {
            return ((i - 15) * 50) + 20;
        }


    })
    .attr("y", function(d,i)
        if (d <= 15) {
            return startLine;
        } else {
            return startLine + 50 + 20;
        }
    })
    .attr("fill","cornflowerblue")
    .on("click", handleMouseClick)
    .on("mouseover", handleMouseOver)
    .on("mouseout", handleMouseOut);

svg.selectAll("text")
    .data(textData)
    .enter()
    .append("text")
    .attr("text-anchor","middle")
    .attr("font-family","Open Sans")
    .attr("fill","black")
    .text(function(d)
        return d;
    })
    .attr("x", function(d, i)
        return (i * 50) + 20;
    })
    .attr("y", 110);

function handleMouseOver(d,i) {
```

Having defined a variable to hold the drawing, let's create some rectangles. How many? As many as there are elements in the data *array. The d3 command* data()*loads the array into memory. Now add a "rect". Assign attributes (h, w) just to each rect as created.*

Position on the screen? X axis is horizontal; y is vertical. The anonymous function, called function()*, accepts two built-in parameters -* d *(for datum) which is each element in the array one-by-one (d) and its position in the array (0, 1, 2, 3, ... n). This is what* i *stands for. The* if *statement determines where to position the rect based on its # in the array (the "data" array).*

Like all HTML elements, we can add color attribute. Mouse Events: *when the end-user clicks, mouses over, or mouse moves out, call the function; e.g.,* on("click", *calls a function (defined below) called* handleMouseClick

Besides adding rects to the svg, we can add text!
Here the text data come from the textData *array*
As before, enter() *to load the data into memory*
What do we want to draw? We wanna draw text.
Position the letters in the middle of the space.
Set the font attribute to "Open Sans"
Set the color of the font to black
What text to say? Each time the d *is called it is replaced by the value from* data, *so "A", "B", "C" ...*

Here the x attribute is assigned to the preceding item created - the text *(and not the rect).*

When the end-user moves the mouse over each rect the

```
        d3.select(this).attr("fill","orange")
}
function handleMouseOut(d,i)
        d3.select(this).attr("fill","cornflowerblue")
}
function handleMouseClick(d,i)
        d3.select(this).attr("fill","red")
        var x = document.getElementById("infoBox");
        if (x.style.display === "none") {
            x.style.display = "block";
        } else
            x.style.display = "none";
        }
}
</script>
</body></html>
```

This demo (figure 4.6) is the above script. The second demo (figure 4.7) shows how such squares could be applied.

Most Popular Resource Services by Department

FIGURE 4.6 One display of a .json data set. *Courtesy of the author*

Services by Year

1993 (1)

Resource Type	Slavic Collections
Unit	Non-English Collection
Value	$871,530,324

2001 (2)
2002 (2)
2003 (2)
2004 (1)
2005 (2)

FIGURE 4.7 Revised display of the same data set, after the end user's mouse-click. *Courtesy of the author*

Example 2

We work in a rare book room and want to display the timeline of some of our collections (figures 4.8 and 4.9). Here we're practicing with a *Hamlet* timeline . . . this is far from finished! Let's see what we want—a banner, images from the collection, a way to capture mouse clicks to change pictures, and to change text on the screen. We need to add the actual timeline and determine what events we want to display, the types of events, resources, and more. It would be best to store those data in a .json file. But for the moment, we'll build the previous experience with mouse-over, mouse-out, onclick, and introduce text.

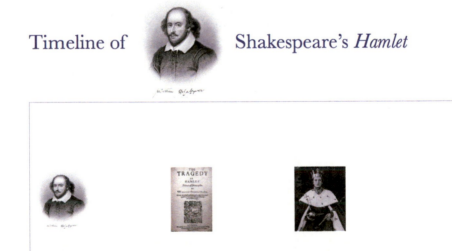

Timeline of Shakespeare's *Hamlet*

FIGURE 4.8 A first draft of applying InfoVis to literature. *Courtesy of the author*

Timeline of Shakespeare's *Hamlet*

I am the Man!

FIGURE 4.9 Mousing over to change the image and start to tell a story. *Courtesy of the author*

Here are the source code examples used in this lab:

```
<!DOCTYPE html>
<html>
<!-- HOW TO SHOW AN IMAGE WITH
D3 -->
<head>
<style>
body { padding: 10px;
    font-family: "Baskerville", serif;
}
#bannerHeading { font-family: inherit;
    font-size: 32px;
    color: midnightblue;
}
</style>
<script src="d3.v4.min.js"></script>      A different version of the d3 library
</head>
<body>

<div id="bannerHeading">Timeline of <img align="middle" width="150px" src="Shakespeare.jpg">
Shakespeare&rsquo;s <i>Hamlet</i></div>

<script>

var data = ["Shakespeare.jpg","hamlet.jpg",      These 2 lines could (should) be in a .json format.
"hamlet2.jpg"];
var textData = ["I am the Man!","Finally in print.","Who is that?"];
```

```
var cx, cy = 200;

var svg = d3.select("body")
    .append("svg")
    .style("border","1px solid silver")
    .attr("width",800)
    .attr("height",600);

svg.selectAll("g")
    .data(data)
    .enter()
    .append('g')
    .attr("width", 300)
    .attr("height",300)
    .append("svg:image")
    .attr("xlink:href",function(d,i)
        return d; })

    .attr("width",100)
    .attr("height",100)
    .attr("x", function(d,i)
        return i * 200 )
    .attr("y",100)
    .on("click", handleMouseClick)
    .on("mouseover", handleMouseOver)
    .on("mouseout", handleMouseOut);

var t = svg.append("text")
    .attr("x",25)
    .attr("y",25)
    .text("hello")
    .attr("font-family","sans-serif")
    .attr("font-size","14px")
    .attr("fill","olive");
function handleMouseOver(d, i) {
    d3.select(this).attr("xlink:href","elizabethfirst.jpg");
}
function handleMouseOut(d, i) {
    d3.select(this).attr("xlink:href",function(d,i)
        return d; })
    t.text("");
}

function handleMouseClick(d,i)
    var coordinates = [0,0];
    coordinates = d3.mouse(this);
    var mx = coordinates[0];
    var my = coordinates[1];
    // alert("MOUSE CLICK x,y? "+mx+","+my+" d is "+d);
```

Important! To draw images we need a graphics container. That container is usually called g. Then we attach the display to that container, which, of course, is attached to the svg defined above, which is attached to the body. The "bounding box" - or area around the image.

We tell d3 to append a graphic (in an svg container, of type image. We use an xlink (XML link technology) and tell it to pretend to be on the Net and return whatever image is referenced in the data array. We can use URLs, too!
These width and height refer only to the size of the image that happens to be an a g container of 300x300.

As before, what to do if the user clicks or mouses over...

This would be different is we used .json, but for the moment let's add some text as before.

A placeholder just for testing. Good idea.

Whatever the image is that the mouse is over now (this image) *let's swap the original image for a new one.*

Just for testing - let's find out where the mouse is!

```
        t.text(textData[i]);
        /* for D3 v4
```
Change the displayed text by using lines from textData array.
Not tested - this is for the next version of d3

```
        var x = d3.event.pageX - document.getElementById(<id-of-your-svg>).getBoundingClientRect().x +
10
        var y = d3.event.pageY - document.getElementById(<id-of-your-svg>).getBoundingClientRect().y +
10
        */

    }
</script>
<p>&copy;2018 <i>Friends of Hamlet</i>.</p>
</body>
</html>
```

All done!
Keep in touch with our friends.

This is Demo 1:

```
<!DOCTYPE html>
<html><head><title>Box Test</title>
<script src="d3.v4.min.js"></script>
    <style>
    #infoBox {
        position: absolute;
        border-radius: 5px;
        background-color: olive;
        color: white;
        padding: 10px;
        font-size: 10px;
        text-align: center;
        top: 120px;
        left: 40%;
        z-index: 2;
        }
    </style>
</head>
<body onload="hideBox()">

<div id="infoBox">This is the info box.</div>

<script>
    function hideBox() {
        document.getElementById("infoBox").style.display = "none";
    }
</script>

<script>
    var w = 20;
    var h = 20;
```

```
    var startLine = 100;
    var padding = 5;
    var data = [1,2,3,4,5,6,7,8,9,10,11,12,13,14,15,16,17,18,19,20];
    var textData =
["A","B","C","D","E","F","G","H","I","J","K","L","M","N","O","P","Q","R","S","T","U"];

    // create SVG element
    var svg = d3.select("body")
        .append("svg")
        .style("border","1px solid silver")
        .attr("width", 800)
        .attr("height", 600);

    svg.selectAll("rect")
        .data(data)
        .enter()
        .append("rect")
        .attr("height", w)
        .attr("width",h)
        .attr("x", function(d, i) {
            if (d <= 15) {
                return (i * 50) + 20;
            } else {
                return ((i - 15) * 50) + 20;
            }
        })
        .attr("y", function(d,i) {
            if (d <= 15) {
                return startLine;
            } else {
                return startLine + 50 + 20;
            }
        })
        .attr("fill","cornflowerblue")
        .on("click", handleMouseClick)
        .on("mouseover", handleMouseOver)
        .on("mouseout", handleMouseOut);

    svg.selectAll("text")
        .data(textData)
        .enter()
        .append("text")
        .attr("text-anchor","middle")
        .attr("font-family","Open Sans")
        .attr("fill","black")
        .text(function(d) {
            return d;
        })
        .attr("x", function(d, i) {
```

```
          return (i * 50) + 20;
       })
       .attr("y", 110);

    function handleMouseOver(d,i) {
       d3.select(this).attr("fill","orange")
    }
    function handleMouseOut(d,i) {
       d3.select(this).attr("fill","cornflowerblue")
    }
    function handleMouseClick(d,i) {
       d3.select(this).attr("fill","red")
       var x = document.getElementById("infoBox");
       if (x.style.display === "none") {
          x.style.display = "block";
       } else {
          x.style.display = "none";
       }
    }
    </script>
  </body>
</html>
```

More Complex Examples

The companion website offers an entire suite of the most popular interactive information visualizations.

REFERENCES

Benoît, G. (2005). Data mining. In B. Cronin (Ed.), *Annual Review of Information Science and Technology* (ARIST), vol. 36 (pp. 265–310). Medford, NJ: Wiley.

Berger, J. (1972). *Ways of seeing*. London: Penguin.

Bertin, J. (1967). *Sémiologie graphique. Les diagrammes, les réseaux, les cartes.* Paris/La Haye, Mouton; Paris: Gauthier-Villars.

Bertin, J. (1977). *La graphique et le traitement graphique de l'information.* Paris: Flammarion.

Keim, D. A. (2002, January). Information visualization and visual data mining. *IEEE Transactions on Visualization and Computer Graphics, 8*(1), 1–8.

Littleton, K., & Whitelock, D. (22 Jan. 2007). The negotiation and co-construction of meaning and understanding within a postgraduate online community. *Learning, media and technology, 30*(2), 147–64.

Mozilla Developers Network. (2018). Introduction to the DOM. Retrieved February 8, 2018, from https://developer.mozilla.org/en-US/docs/Web/API/Document_Object_Model/Introduction

Murray, Scott. (2013). *Interactive information visualization for the web.* Sebastopol, CA: O'Reilly Media. (Online version: https://www.oreilly.com/).

w3schools. (2018). The HTML DOM (Document Object Model). Retrieved February 8, 2018, from https://www.w3schools.com/js/js_htmldom.asp

## CHAPTER 5

The Thought behind Creating a Visualization

In this chapter we raise a variety of points about how we think about creating a visualization. The theme is integrated with literature from across perspectives in the InfoVis field, and also hooks into related areas in the arts. Student case studies are presented to demonstrate how a person realizes his or her idea. Finally, this chapter continues with samples and code for some common techniques. Determining what kind of visualization to create depends on a number of constraints and opportunities. The designer's preferences and work domain seem to be among the most vital, so let's start here.

Graphic designers—and here we include data and information-visualization specialists—cannot help but favor compositions and color pallets they feel most comfortable with because the colors "speak" to them or because the colors are trending. For instance, there are many websites detailing predefined color schemes, such as Color Hunt (https://colorhunt.co/), ColourLovers (http://www.colourlovers .com/), Design Seeds (https://www.design-seeds.com/), Paletton (http://paletton .com/), and Color Palettes [http://colorpalettes.net/), to name a few. *Communication Arts*, the leading professional graphic design journal, hosts galleries, competitions, and interactive design, notably the "Color Chart: Reinventing Color—1950 to Today" (https://www.commarts.com/webpicks/color-chart-reinventing-color -1950-to-today), and "Soothsayer of Color" (https://www.commarts.com/columns /soothsayer-of-color).

Third-party visualization applications, such as R's ggplot, Tableau, Python, and Bokeh (https://github.com/bokeh/bokeh), have templates into which the data are inserted, because these applications are primarily for *data* analysis, not visualizations. We need to notice when these software apps provide little to no opportunity to tailor the style to our needs. Color choices are usually predetermined and fixed. We wish to avoid shaping the client or intended audience for the visualization, instead of the other way around.

Work domains follow trends in a given industry and creating the iconography and representation colors, the way "medicine" is represented by a red caduceus. Line plots are a common enough way to visualize statistical data, so line plot templates are naturally a first choice when exploring visualization. Applying familiar trends promote quick reception of the design and interpretation of the results by people in the field. A judiciously designed alternative to presenting graphics engages the end user on a different cognitive plane by shaking up the expected visuals and data presentation that forces an internal dialogue to establish meaningfulness from the design. Researchers in the InfoVis domain make a conscious effort to reach across domains from mathematics to history, suggesting opportunities for interdisciplinary work in digital humanities and user experience, among others (Burkhard et al., 2007).

Setting aside these points for the moment, if we start from scratch creating an interactive information visualization, the designer must weigh his or her knowledge of design principles and capabilities of the output device to present the design as intended:

- Audience expectations
- Types of interactivity with the end user
- Properties of the data themselves
- The domain or topic being studied
- The purpose of the InfoVis
- The myriad aesthetic decisions associated with any graphic design

Stated differently, we do not want to adopt blindly, and without reflection on our choices, a visual foundation, nor the technology that do not contribute to presenting, explaining, and exploring data in a way that it supports truthful interpretation and stimulates insight.

HOW TO THINK ABOUT THE DESIGN?

How to approach a visualization problem? Several options exist, and doubtless more will be created as InfoVis evolves. A shorthand way of thinking about this is how one might approach from a data-centric, user-centric, visual-centric starting point, to arrive at a holistic communications-centric approach integrating the other three:

- Data-centric
- User-centric
- Visual-centric
- Communications-centric

Data-Centric Approach

The problem-solving approach favored in the big data/data science realm is data-centric. This is likely because of the similarities between traditional data- and text-mining activities that incorporate visualizing results for exploration and explanation. This field contributes to receptiveness by institutions and the public to very large datasets and the computational infrastructure that provides the data. For data scientists, however, the ultimate interest is using visuals to help *chart* the data, as opposed to interacting with them. The emphasis is on large datasets and machine learning.

The data science literature suggests a couple of trends. In *Beautiful Visualization* (Steele & Illinsky, 2010), *Atlas of Science* (Börner, 2016), and *Atlas of Knowledge* (Börner, 2014), we can read a number of "how I did it" type articles from the programmers' point of view.

Another is the preference for the graphing tools that are part of statistical packages. Munzner's *Visualization Analysis and Design* (2014) is a notable example of the computer science camp exploring visualizations but in a novel dialect, describing visual primitives as "marks" and design as "channels."

User-Centric Approach

Arguably, this is the traditional realm of the librarian and some computer and information scientists. The role of the data—from their collection, preparation, and technical specifics—are of less importance to the UX (user experience) designer. Interestingly, research at the intersection of visualization and user-centric work has grown exponentially in the past decades. Some include depictions of everyday life (Pousman, Stasko, & Mateas, 2007), browsing photo collections (Moghaddam, Tian, Lesh, Shen, & Huang, 2004), and intriguing cause-and-effect on design using Gephi (Jacomy, Venturini, Heymann, & Bastian, 2014).

A hybrid UX and empirical science blend is represented by Ware's *Visual Thinking* (2008) and many articles by Jeff Heer (see Heer, Viégas, & Wattenberg, 2007). The former starts with the biology of vision and measurement of human reaction; the latter, with how visuals prompt online discussion.

Visual-Centric Approach

The visual-centric approach is the historical and contemporary information graphic enterprise. Here are tied the fundamental issues of graphic design (composition, color, typography/text), the impact of the printing/display media, the history of illustration, the impacts of tools used to create the graphics, and studies in visual literacy.

We find an astonishingly large and broad literature of histories of the various components mentioned above relating to the ever-evolving visual language. Works by Drucker (2014) and Tufte (1990) represent the "how visuals are used in knowledge" stream of thought. Extremely popular works, they demonstrate the public interest in the history and applications of visuals in recording knowledge, sharing, and teaching. Meirelles's *Design for Information* (2013) takes the step into the data-centric world, but from the perspective of a graphic designer.

Visual-centric work probably has the broadest range of investigation. Rudolf Arnheim's research underlines our interest in the power of our perceptions to transform the viewer's understanding and reasoning. In *Art and Visual Perception* (1974), *Visual Thinking* (1969), and *The Power of the Center: A Study of Composition in the Visual Arts* (1982), he argues that people reason with patterns, shapes, and colors, and that how we see the world while trying to understand these visual elements changes our perception of meaningfulness. Eagleton's *The Ideology of the Aesthetic* (1991) provides an informative, intriguing critical survey of philosophic perspectives of aesthetics, ethics, and politics.

Communications-Centric Approach

The communications-centric perspective considers first and foremost that the purpose of the visualization is to foster a sustainable discourse, even if that be the individual viewer's unarticulated mental activity. Interactivity as communication fosters

- long-term engagement with the visualization based on the aesthetic qualities;
- understanding the interplay between the data that are the foundation and their graphic representation's placement, color, and similarities/differences;
- interacting with the two bullet points above to arrive at a conclusion, or some new knowledge;
- helping a viewer take further action (i.e., make a person aware of the phenomenon, knowledgeable, and hence "being informed"); and
- providing a rationale for conclusion so that the viewer can articulate the reasons for his/her decisions

We see the components of visualizations, data, audience, aesthetics, and the cognitive engagement of the viewer as she or he interprets the symbols into a candidate significance. Working both in a design by interacting with the data (such as drilling down, brushing, revealing the raw data), and engaging in a dialog (internally or orally with other people), the candidate interpretations' truthfulness, validity, and applicability are brought out. The result is simultaneously both an objective data-driven meaning and a socially constructed one.

USE CASES

The best way to develop InfoVis skills is to practice them. Below are a few use cases that explain how the designer of the visualization came to a solution. Moving from static charts to interactive visualization for information introduces more layers of display, more data, and interactive opportunities that, in the end, reflect a truthful telling of the story of the data and multiple stories as end users ask their questions through the graphic.

Developing a design is an interactive process. Some authors believe that it is the data that dictate the design; others advise about the designers' (or clients') interests, such as Abela's "Chart Suggestions—a Thought-Starter" (figure 5.1).

I think creating the chart design requires simultaneous hermeneutic understanding of the data, client, and visual possibilities. For example, identify the following as you sketch up your wireframe.

- Audience: Is the audience interested in, or expecting, the visual to explain, explore, and/or discover new knowledge? How long a time frame will the audience invest? What is the necessary level of knowledge about the topic and about data in general?

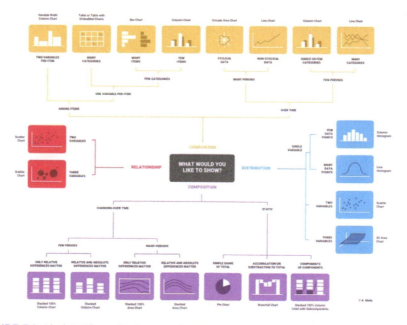

CHART SUGGESTIONS - A THOUGHT-STARTER

FIGURE 5.1 Abela's Thought-Starter chart. One model (of many) about how to decide what chart type. *Based on www.ExtremePresentation.com, ©2009 A. Abela, a.v.abela@gmail.com*

- Output: Are there any impacts of the screen/monitor that affect the design and the interactivity of the design?
- Aesthetic appeal: What's the affective quality to be expressed?
- Composition:
  - Color pallet: How much does color suggesting grouping, subgroups, reveal unexpected events?
  - Display typography: Can viewers identify easily the title, subfields, and main context by typeface?
  - How does drilling down, zooming, brushing, pop-ups, and white space affect the visuals' legibility? For instance, mouse-over for details-on-demand displays alters the graphic design, perhaps affecting legibility.
  - Color density and color model:
    - Analogous
    - Complementary
- Data:
  - Number of variables to be displayed (univariate, bivariate, or multivariate)
  - Calculated data to be created before visualization?
  - Recalculate data during interactivity?
  - Number of data types to be displayed?
    - Relationship of variables among the data?
  - Time-based?
    - Single period?
    - Few periods?
    - Many periods?
  - Geographic?

Is the visualization at first intended to demonstrate relationships, comparison, difference/similarities or other trends? Should we emphasize the data, we might ask about the variables and features:

- Raw data: show the variables in the graphic with access to source data
- Features: variables constructed from the raw data, for instance, salary trends as a feature of individual salary data points
- Target variable: visually suggest what data are trying to be predicted
- Predictive variables: usually covariates; data used to predict trends from features, such as credit history and vehicles owned
- Predictive model: demonstrate the predictive model accepting raw data and features, and then changing the visualization to suggest the story of the changing trend

VISUALIZATIONS ON THE JOB: PART 1

Surf the web, check the library, and read tech and business journals to see countless graphics, charts, and visualizations. Presenting an exhaustive list and demonstration of every visualization style would not be fruitful. Instead, we'll explore designs that are both recognizable and fairly easy to implement in d3.

Visit the online companion site (https://infovis.bix.digital/index.html) to learn how to create the visualizations for display in a browser. There you will also find the entire documentation and coding for your own institution to establish a new InfoVis service for your patrons.

Gallery of Visualization Examples and Specifics

The examples here are fully documented on the companion website's demonstration folder. The gallery is most useful when reading the data source and the source code to clarify in your own mind the interplay of the two.

A how-to: Responding to end user input is vital to our visualization activities. Below are three detailed examples, showing the relationships of HTML, CSS, d3, and JavaScript. The first is an almost line-by-line explanation of the coding to create and to respond to a grid. The second is a popular version of a tree map. In this example, we create the HTML page and read data in from a flat file.

Example 1: Static Hierarchical Tree

Start with an elementary hierarchical tree (figure 5.2). There are no interactive options and color decisions; just practicing reading a .json file.

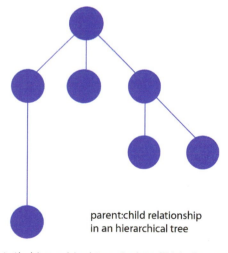

parent:child relationship
in an hierarchical tree

FIGURE 5.2 A static hierarchical tree (using d3.js). *Courtesy of the author*

```html
<!DOCTYPE html>
<meta charset="utf-8">
<head>
    <title>Tree layout</title>
</head>

<style>
.node {
    fill: steelblue;
    stroke: none;
}
.link {
    fill: none;
    stroke: #ccc;
    stroke-width: 1px;
}
</style>
<body>
    <h2>An hierarchical tree </h2>
    <svg width="700" height="500">
            <g transform="translate(5, 5)">
            <g class="nodes"></g>
        </g>
    </svg>

    <script src="js/d3.v4.min.js"></script>
    <script>
```

Define the color we want for each member of the hierarchy ("node").

Define the color for the links (or "edges").

Important! First define an object to hold the drawing ("svg") and assign the attributes of width & height.

Define a graphic object, by convention called "g".

Load the d3 library (here in a subfolder called js).

```javascript
var data;
// var treeLayout;
// var root;
d3.json("data/networkdata1.json", function(json) {
    data = json;
    var treeLayout = d3.tree()
        .size([500, 300])

    var root = d3.hierarchy(data)

    treeLayout(root)

// Nodes
d3.select('svg g.nodes')
    .selectAll('circle.node')
    .data(root.descendants())
    .enter()
    .append('circle')
    .classed('node', true)

    .attr('cx', function(d) {return d.x;})
    .attr('cy', function(d) {return d.y;})
    .attr('r', 12);


// Link
d3.select('svg g.links')
    .selectAll('line.link')
    .data(root.links())
    .enter()
    .append('line')
    .classed('link', true)
    .attr('x1', function(d) {return d.source.x;})
    .attr('y1', function(d) {return d.source.y;})
    .attr('x2', function(d) {return d.target.x;})
    .attr('y2', function(d) {return d.target.y;});


});
    </script>
</body>
</html>
```

d3 has a subclass called .json() that understands how to read and parse .json file. Define a tree (using d3's tree()subclass, using the .json data just loaded

Identify the starting point to read the data as "root" associated with the "data" variable, holding the .json data. Automatically build the tree in memory.

Tell d3 to select all of the nodes (that belong to "g", which in their turn belong to "svg"). Each one ("selectAll")...

The .enter() is as if we typed the data by hand. Each node data is now translated into an SVG circle and added to the DOM tree. The attributes (.attr) are assigned next. The anonymous function(d) accepts "d" that is an automatically created

variable by d3 and holds the loaded values as if in a for... loop. Incrementally treating each datum from the file (even though we can't see them unless we look at the browser's "console" window).

Now tell d3 to add the edges to the nodes.

The anonymous function automatically has a parameter called "d" [for datum]. The function matches the node (created above) coordinates (source.x, source.y, to target.x, target.y) the ends of the lines (edges) linking them.

Example 2: Grid

In this how-to, we create a grid system, then we track where the end user clicks by showing which *x, y* coordinate box was selected, and the box number's ID (figures 5.3A and 5.3B). These are important to capture in the script so that we can design a reaction, such as cause a dialog box or a <div> to show the data.

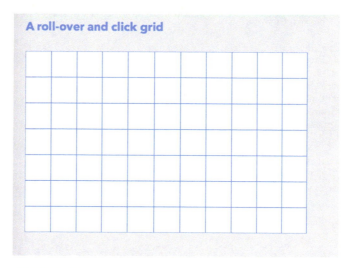

FIGURE 5.3A A demo grid, preparing for interactivity (using d3.js). *Courtesy of the author*

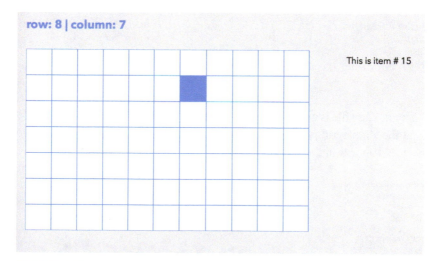

FIGURE 5.3B Responding to on_mouseover and on_mouseclick methods (using d3.js). *Courtesy of the author*

This example is typical in that we need (a) an .html page, (b) a .css file, (c) a link to a version of d3.js, and (d) optionally, data files and additional .js files. Starting with the .html page, let's read the source.

```
<!DOCTYPE html>
<html lang="en">
<head>
    <meta charset="utf-8"/ >
    <title>d3 | Mouseover Grid</title>
    <style>
        #boxData    {
            position: absolute;
            top: 100px;
            left: 520px;
            font-family "Open Sans", "Avenir Next", sans-serif;
            font-size: 14px;
            color: black;
        }
    </style>
    <link rel="stylesheet" href="box.css">

    <script src="d3.v3.min.js">
    </script>

</head>

<header>
    <h4 id="grid-ref">A roll-over and click grid</h4>
</header>

<section id='grid'></section>
<div id="boxData"></div>

<script src="simplegrid.js">
</script>
</body>
</html>
```

A div with ID "boxData"; show mouse click data here.

The stylesheet ("box.css"). In the same folder as the .html page.
Link to d3 (version 3 in this case); also in same folder.

Register the grid section in the DOM.
Register the boxID div in the DOM.

Here's the work: the simplegrid.js will load here and draw the grid.

The box.css file is available on the companion site, as is the d3.vs.min.js. Let's look at the simplegrid.js file. While the commands are listed in a separate file, the same could appear in the source .html file.

```
/* this is simplegrid.js */
var square = 40,
    w = 450,
    h = 280;

// create the svg
var svg = d3.select('#grid').append('svg')
    .attr({
        width: w,
        height: h
    });
```

Define the area that will hold the grid.

Create a variable, coincidentally labeled "svg". Next select the #grid section, created in the .html page. Now we append an actual scalable vector graphic object to the grid area. Using the .attr (for "attribute"), assign the width and height.

```
// calculate number of rows and columns
var squaresRow = Math.round(w / square);
var squaresColumn = Math.round(h / square);

// loop over number of columns
for (var n = 0; n < squaresColumn; n++) {

    // create each set of rows
    var rows = svg.selectAll('rect' + ' .row-' + (n + 1))
        .data(d3.range(squaresRow))
        .enter().append('rect')
        .on("click", function() {




            var coords=d3.mouse(this);

            alert("hit coords "+coords);

    })
    .attr({
        class: function(d, i) {
            return 'square row-' + (n + 1) + ' ' + 'col-' + (i + 1);
        },
        id: function(d, i) {
            return 's-' + (n + 1) + (i + 1);
        },
        width: square,
        height: square,

        x: function(d, i) {
            return i * square;
        },
        y: n * square,
        fill: '#fff',
        stroke: 'cornflowerblue'
    });

    // test with some feedback

    var test = rows.on('mouseover', function (d, i) {
        d3.select('#grid-ref').text(function() {
                showBoxData(n + i + 2);
            return 'row: ' + (n + 1) +
            ' | ' + 'column: ' + (i + 1);
        });
        d3.selectAll('.square').attr('fill', 'white');
        d3.select(this).attr('fill', 'cornflowerblue');
    });



}

function showBoxData(x) {
```

Rather than read in data (as we would here), this script just calculates the number of rows & columns ("data points").

Just as we would with data read in from a file using d3, we loop over every data point incrementally - from the first to the last in the array.

The .data is a d3 command to identify the actual source data and which loads the data into memory. Here we ask d3 to determine the range (values) of the data. The enter() function acts as if we, the user, pressed the "enter" key to load the data. Upon entering the data, we append a rectangle ("rect") to the svg object. Finally, let's add the ability to "listen" to the mouse clicks. The "on" triggers the rectangle to "listen" to the click; The "click" is one of the many actions we can listen to - equivalent to JavaScript's ... onclick=myFunction();

Capture the screen's x,y coordinates of the click (in pixels).
Use JavaScript's own alert() function and pass the mouse coordinates captured by d3.

Color can be identified by hex or html color names.

Here we capture a different mouse behavior: mouseover. When the mouse hovers over a square, create an anonymous function (called "function()). The d "datum" [a d3 automatic parameter]; the i means "iterator [a d3 automatic counter].

Now that we know where the mouse is hovering, we iterate through the entire array of squares and change the color to "white"; the square over which the mouse is positioned is identified by the keyword "this" - informing the script to refer to itself and look the current square - hence "Select 'this' square and change the color to cornflower blue."

And we can create our already-familiar JavaScript functions.

```
document.getElementById("boxData").innerHTML = "This is item # "+x;
```

}

The "boxData" div created in the .html page is now used to display the number of the square. The number is passed as "x" to the showBoxData() function. The x is calculated from showBoxData(n + i + 2); above.

/* end of the script */

Example 3: An Interactive Tree Map

In figure 5.4A and 5.4B, we see typical tree layouts. The colors are arbitrary. There are two user options: to show the data based on the size of the data or the count of the data. The squares are labeled based on their place in the hierarchy of the source data file, a .json file. Let's review the structure of .json here and then the script: .json files are *very* touchy! One] or } out of place, and the file will not load. Study the structure of this file. Even though the .json file is readable without all of the indents and line breaks, adding them helps identify parent and child subsets so that we can debug. Note, too, that there are two variable names in this demo. The name of the var is happily "name", separated by a : and then a value. Children nodes are wrapped in [ ] pair. Each individual data pairing is marked with { and }.

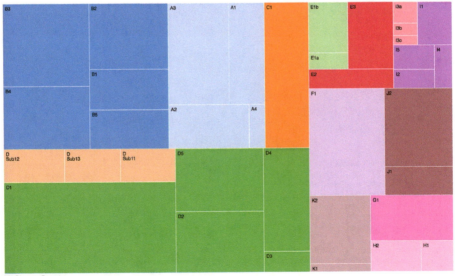

FIGURE 5.4A Treemap: The data are distributed by size (using d3.js). *Courtesy of the author*

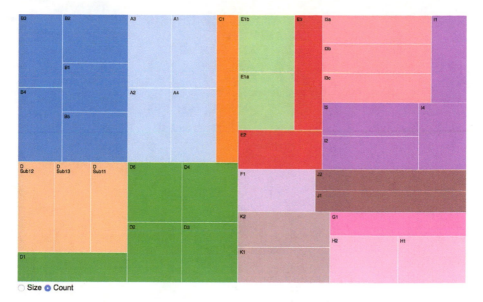

○ Size ● Count

FIGURE 5.4B The data are rearranged based on the underlying counts (using d3.js).
Courtesy of the author

This file is named "treedemo.json".

```
{
    "name": "myroot",
    "children": [
    {
        "name": "demosets",
        "children": [
        {
            "name": "A",
            "children": [
                {"name": "A1", "size": 3938},
                {"name": "A2", "size": 3812},
                {"name": "A3", "size": 6714},
                {"name": "A4", "size": 743}
            ]
        },
        {
            "name": "B",
            "children": [
                {"name": "B1", "size": 3534},
                {"name": "B2", "size": 5731},
                {"name": "B3", "size": 7840},
                {"name": "B4", "size": 5914},
```

```
                    {"name": "B5", "size": 3416}
                ]
            },
            {
                "name": "C",
                "children": [
                    {"name": "C1", "size": 7074}
                ]
            }
            ]
        },
        {
            "name": "D",
            "children": [
                {"name": "D1", "size": 17010},
                {"name": "D2", "size": 5842},
                {

                  "name": "DSub1",
                  "children": [
                      {"name": "DSub11", "size": 1983},
                      {"name": "DSub12", "size": 2202},
                      {"name": "DSub13", "size": 2042}
                  ]
                },
                {"name": "D3", "size": 1041},
                {"name": "D4", "size": 5176},
                {"name": "D5", "size": 6006}
            ]
        },
        {
            "name": "E",
            "children": [
            {
                "name": "E1",
                "children": [
                    {"name": "E1a", "size": 721},
                    {"name": "E1b", "size": 2220}
                ]
            },
        {"name": "E2", "size": 1759},
        {"name": "E3", "size": 3322}
            ]
        },
        {
            "name": "F",
            "children": [
```

```json
            {"name": "F1", "size": 8833}
        ]
    },
    {
        "name": "G",
        "children": [
            {"name": "G1", "size": 4116}
        ]
    },
    {

        "children": [
            {"name": "H1", "size": 1082},
            {"name": "H2", "size": 1681}
        ]
    },
    {
        "name": "I",
        "children": [
            {"name": "I1", "size": 1616},
            {"name": "I2", "size": 843},
            {
                "name": "I3",
                "children": [
                    {"name": "I3a", "size": 593},
                    {"name": "I3b", "size": 330},
                    {"name": "I3c", "size": 264}
                ]
            },
            {"name": "I4", "size": 843},
            {"name": "I5", "size": 1101}
        ]
    },
    {
        "name": "J",
        "children": [
            {"name": "J1", "size": 2105},
            {"name": "J2", "size": 5833}
        ]
    },
    {
        "name": "K",
        "children": [
            {"name": "K1", "size": 540},
            {"name": "K2", "size": 4540}
        ]
    }
    ]
}
```

```
<!DOCTYPE html>
<style>
form {
    font-family: "Open Sans", Helvetica, Arial, sans-serif;
}

svg {                                            For the svg to be added, set the font size.
    font: 10px sans-serif;
}
</style>

<svg width="960" height="570"></svg>            Define the size of the svg object.
<form>                                           This form hosts the radio buttons for user-input.

    <label><input type="radio" name="mode" value="sumBySize" checked> Size</label>
    <label><input type="radio" name="mode" value="sumByCount"> Count</label>
</form>

<script src="d3.v4.min.js"></script>            Notice we're using a different version of d3.  Always check
<script>                                         yours.

var svg = d3.select("svg"),                      As above, follow the convention of naming both var and
    width = +svg.attr("width"),                  object "svg".
    height = +svg.attr("height");
                                                  Below is just a colorful effect when swapping between sum
                                                  sizes.

var fader = function(color) { return d3.interpolateRgb(color, "#fff")(0.2); },
    color = d3.scaleOrdinal(d3.schemeCategory20.map(fader)),
    format = d3.format(",d");

var treemap = d3.treemap()                       d3 has a function called treemap() to facilitate creating the
    .tile(d3.treemapResquarify)                  tree.
    .size([width, height])                       determine a width/height for each square; revise based on
                                                  the data
    .round(true)                                 round the values to an integer.  better to draw boxes this
                                                  way.
    .paddingInner(1);                            Add some padding (1 pixel) between colored squares of the
                                                  tree.
d3.json("treedemo.json", function(error, data) { Our source data is in this .json file.  If the file is not
    if (error) throw error;                      readable, throw an "exception" or error; otherwise, load
                                                  the data starting at the root.

    var root = d3.hierarchy(data)
        .eachBefore(function(d) { d.data.id = (d.parent ? d.parent.data.id + "." : "") +
            d.data.name; })
        .sum(sumBySize)
        .sort(function(a, b) { return b.height - a.height || b.value - a.value; });

    treemap(root);                               Data loaded - create tree starting with root.
```

The below variables define the properties for each of the cells (the squares in the tree). The data() and enter() iterate through the data - sequentially starting at the first value through the bottom of the file's last value. The "g" refers to the graphic object.

```
var cell = svg.selectAll("g")
    .data(root.leaves())
    .enter().append("g")
```

The "enter" assigned the data to each "g" which has properties of an x,y location [below d.x0 and d.y0]; and ID and a fill color.

```
    .attr("transform", function(d) { return "translate(" + d.x0 + "," + d.y0 + ")"; });


cell.append("rect")
        .attr("id", function(d) { return d.data.id; })
        .attr("width", function(d) { return d.x1 - d.x0; })
        .attr("height", function(d) { return d.y1 - d.y0; })
        .attr("fill", function(d) { return color(d.parent.data.id); });

cell.append("clipPath")
        .attr("id", function(d) { return "clip-" + d.data.id; })
    .append("use")
        .attr("xlink:href", function(d) { return "#" + d.data.id; });

cell.append("text")
        .attr("clip-path", function(d) { return "url(#clip-" + d.data.id + ")"; })
    .selectAll("tspan")
        .data(function(d) { return d.data.name.split(/(?=[A-Z][^A-Z])/g); })
    .enter().append("tspan")
        .attr("x", 4)
        .attr("y", function(d, i) { return 13 + i * 10; })
        .text(function(d) { return d; });

cell.append("title")
        .text(function(d) { return d.data.id + "\n" + format(d.value); });

d3.selectAll("input")
        .data([sumBySize, sumByCount], function(d) { return d ? d.name : this.value; })
        .on("change", changed);

var timeout = d3.timeout(function() {
    d3.select("input[value=\"sumByCount\"]")
            .property("checked", true)
            .dispatch("change");
}, 2000);
```

```
    function changed(sum) {
        timeout.stop();

        treemap(root.sum(sum));

        cell.transition()
                .duration(750)
                .attr("transform", function(d) { return "translate(" + d.x0 + "," + d.y0 + ")"; })
            .select("rect")
                .attr("width", function(d) { return d.x1 - d.x0; })
                .attr("height", function(d) { return d.y1 - d.y0; });
    }
});

function sumByCount(d) {
    return d.children ? 0 : 1;
}

function sumBySize(d) {
    return d.size;
}

</script>
/* end of the file */
```

The above coding samples are demonstrated on the companion site. The following graphics are screen images from the project that show how information about the chart, file times, and interactive opportunities meet at the nexus of users and data.

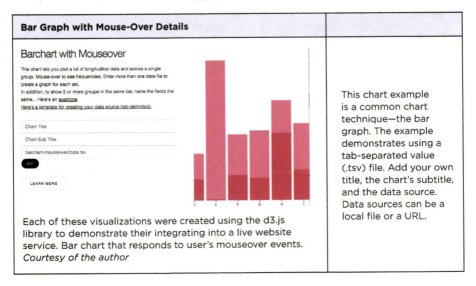

Bar Graph with Mouse-Over Details

Barchart with Mouseover

This chart lets you plot a lot of longitudinal data and across a single group. Mouse-over to see frequencies. Enter more than one data file to create a graph for each set.
In addition, to show 2 or more groups in the same bar, name the fields the same... Here's an example.
Here's a template for creating your data source (tab-delimited).

Chart Title

Chart Sub Title

barchart-mouseover/data.tsv

LEARN MORE

This chart example is a common chart technique—the bar graph. The example demonstrates using a tab-separated value (.tsv) file. Add your own title, the chart's subtitle, and the data source. Data sources can be a local file or a URL.

Each of these visualizations were created using the d3.js library to demonstrate their integrating into a live website service. Bar chart that responds to user's mouseover events. *Courtesy of the author*

Bar Graph with Changeable Series

Bar Chart with Changeable Series

It is useful at times to explore data by dividing the dataset into smaller division. In this example the default is set to 4 series. Altering the # of series of changes the color and size of the chart so you can explore different classification scenarios. Enter your own URL or file name or try this DEMO URL comma-delimited file: (paste in form + select comma) http://web.simmons.edu/~benoit/hu/demodata.txt

[LEARN MORE]

| File name or url, e.g., http://jonesie | # of series: e.g., 4 |

| tab | SUBMIT |

Bar graph with changeable series. *From d3.js*

It is useful at times to explore data by dividing the dataset into smaller divisions. In this example, the default is set to four series. Altering the number of series changes the color and size of the chart so that you can explore different classification scenarios. Enter your own URL or file name or try this DEMO URL comma-delimited file (paste in form + select comma): https://bix.digital/infovis /demos/demodata.txt

In this example, we can select the file data type.

| ✓ Select delimiter |
| comma |
| json |
| tab |
| xml |

End users' data may be comma- or tab-delimited, or in .json or .xml.

Collapsible Tree (Dendogram)

Collapsible Tree

These trees are great for showing the relationships of data and by minimizing/maximizing the tree, viewers investigate the relationships. Enter your own file's URL or press enter to view the demo. Here is an example of the data source file. Download the Excel template for your data.

[LEARN MORE]

| Enter a title |

| And a subtitle |

| https://bix.digital/infovis/demos/collapsibleTree.html |

[GO!]

Dendograms are very useful in time series, hierarchies such as family trees. Getting details on demand for any part of the tree allows presenting a great deal of text data without cluttering the display.

Collapsible trees (using d3.js). *Courtesy of the author*

Choropleth	
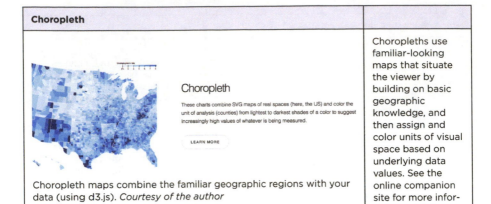 Choropleth maps combine the familiar geographic regions with your data (using d3.js). *Courtesy of the author*	Choropleths use familiar-looking maps that situate the viewer by building on basic geographic knowledge, and then assign and color units of visual space based on underlying data values. See the online companion site for more information and demo choropleths.

Radar Visualization	
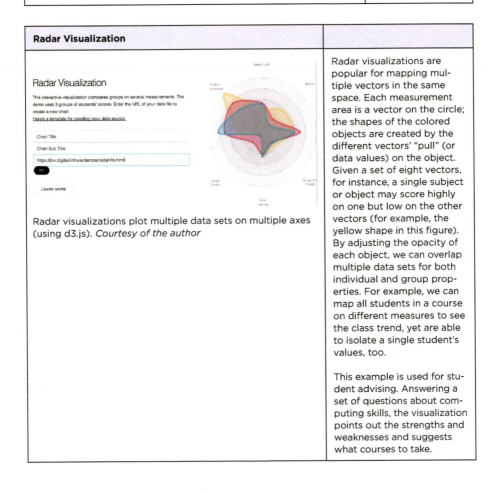 Radar visualizations plot multiple data sets on multiple axes (using d3.js). *Courtesy of the author*	Radar visualizations are popular for mapping multiple vectors in the same space. Each measurement area is a vector on the circle; the shapes of the colored objects are created by the different vectors' "pull" (or data values) on the object. Given a set of eight vectors, for instance, a single subject or object may score highly on one but low on the other vectors (for example, the yellow shape in this figure). By adjusting the opacity of each object, we can overlap multiple data sets for both individual and group properties. For example, we can map all students in a course on different measures to see the class trend, yet are able to isolate a single student's values, too.

This example is used for student advising. Answering a set of questions about computing skills, the visualization points out the strengths and weaknesses and suggests what courses to take. |

Data Table with Lines: Brushable

Data table: lines (using d3.js). *Courtesy of the author*

Data tables with lines are bar graphs. But being able to scroll horizontally to see trends as well as isolating (by "brushing") the data, we can identify individual horizontal trends (as with a line graph) yet also create subgroups on the fly to identify potential trends. In this layout, the lines appear in the upper half, the raw data in the lower half.

Brushing Columns

Longitudinal data (using d3.js). *Courtesy of the author*

Longitudinal graphics plot data and volume such that we can color the trends emphasizing the values above and below a regression line. As with the line graphs, we selectively isolate subsets of the data by "brushing."

Multibrush Visualization

Multibrush visualization (using d3.js). *Courtesy of the author*

Multibrush visualization allows us to compare multiple data sources on two axes, such as volume and time. In this example, five library departments' services, plotted against enrollment, are compared.

Zoomable Pack

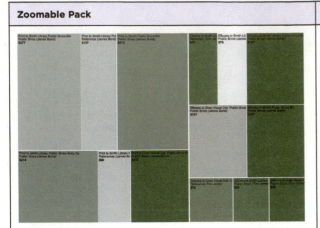

This chart demonstrates multiple clusters, multiple subsets, and a "control panel" for end user interaction (using d3.js). *Courtesy of the author*

Zooming in/out in a visualization has long been a cardinal functionality. In this example, the data are presented as parent-child clusters, with options to double-click on a circle and zoom in to see the subsets in more detail.

(InfoVis-Circles/index .html)

Interactive Treemap

Register-based Visualization

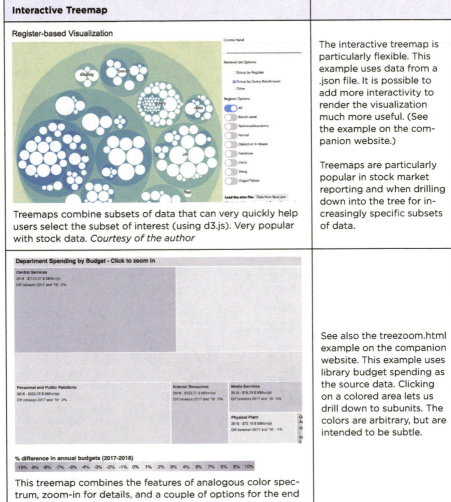

Treemaps combine subsets of data that can very quickly help users select the subset of interest (using d3.js). Very popular with stock data. *Courtesy of the author*

The interactive treemap is particularly flexible. This example uses data from a .json file. It is possible to add more interactivity to render the visualization much more useful. (See the example on the companion website.)

Treemaps are particularly popular in stock market reporting and when drilling down into the tree for increasingly specific subsets of data.

See also the treezoom.html example on the companion website. This example uses library budget spending as the source data. Clicking on a colored area lets us drill down to subunits. The colors are arbitrary, but are intended to be subtle.

This treemap combines the features of analogous color spectrum, zoom-in for details, and a couple of options for the end user to see the raw data values.

Force-Directed with Clickable Images	

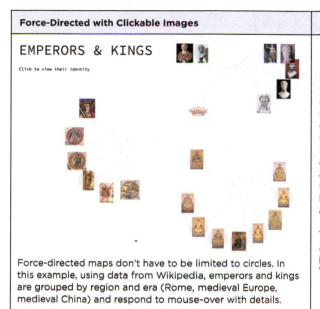

EMPERORS & KINGS

Click to view their identity

Force-directed maps don't have to be limited to circles. In this example, using data from Wikipedia, emperors and kings are grouped by region and era (Rome, medieval Europe, medieval China) and respond to mouse-over with details.

Force-directed graphs are very popular with any kind of relationships—particularly so with text, identifying character relationships, and indeed anything historical. In this example, images are added (for Chinese and Roman emperors and English kings), with mouse behaviors that link to images and web pages.

The data are stored in a .json file with links to Wikipedia pages (forceDirected WithImages.html).

Time Series	

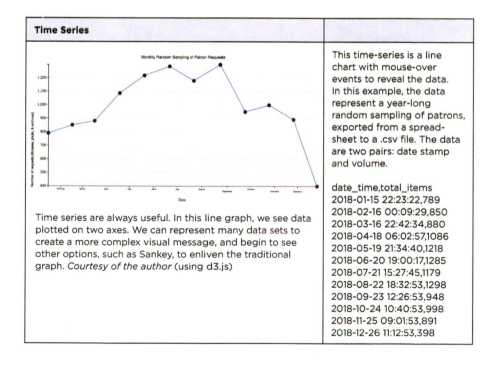

Monthly Random Sampling of Patron Requests

Time series are always useful. In this line graph, we see data plotted on two axes. We can represent many data sets to create a more complex visual message, and begin to see other options, such as Sankey, to enliven the traditional graph. *Courtesy of the author* (using d3.js)

This **time-series** is a line chart with mouse-over events to reveal the data. In this example, the data represent a year-long random sampling of patrons, exported from a spread-sheet to a .csv file. The data are two pairs: date stamp and volume.

date_time,total_items
2018-01-15 22:23:22,789
2018-02-16 00:09:29,850
2018-03-16 22:42:34,880
2018-04-18 06:02:57,1086
2018-05-19 21:34:40,1218
2018-06-20 19:00:17,1285
2018-07-21 15:27:45,1179
2018-08-22 18:32:53,1298
2018-09-23 12:26:53,948
2018-10-24 10:40:53,998
2018-11-25 09:01:53,891
2018-12-26 11:12:53,398

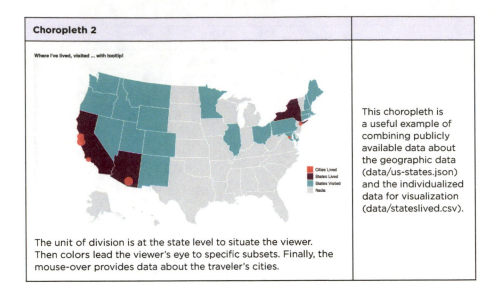

Choropleth 2	
Where I've lived, visited ... with tooltip! Cities Lived States Lived States Visited Nada	This choropleth is a useful example of combining publicly available data about the geographic data (data/us-states.json) and the individualized data for visualization (data/stateslived.csv).
The unit of division is at the state level to situate the viewer. Then colors lead the viewer's eye to specific subsets. Finally, the mouse-over provides data about the traveler's cities.	

The following example demonstrates the choropleth in figure 5.18.

```
<!DOCTYPE html>
<!-- FROM http://bl.ocks.org/michellechandra/0b2ce4923dc9b5809922 -->
<html lang="en">
<head>
<meta charset="utf-8">
<script src="js/d3.v3.min.js"></script>
<link rel="stylesheet" type="text/css" href="citieslived.css">

</head>
<body>
    <h3>Where I've lived, visited ... with tooltip!</h3>

<script type="text/javascript">

/*  This visualization was made possible by modifying code provided by:

Scott Murray, Choropleth example from "Interactive Data Visualization for the Web"
https://github.com/alignedleft/d3-book/blob/master/chapter_12/05_choropleth.html

Malcolm Maclean, tooltips example tutorial
http://www.d3noob.org/2013/01/adding-tooltips-to-d3js-graph.html

Mike Bostock, Pie Chart Legend
http://bl.ocks.org/mbostock/3888852  */
```

```
//Width and height of map
var width = 960;
var height = 500;

// D3 Projection
var projection = d3.geo.albersUsa()
                    .translate([width/2, height/2])   // translate to center of screen
                    .scale([1000]);                    // scale things down so see entire US

// Define path generator
var path = d3.geo.path()          // path generator that will convert GeoJSON to SVG paths
             .projection(projection);   // tell path generator to use albersUsa projection

// Define linear scale for output
var color = d3.scale.linear()

range(["rgb(213,222,217)","rgb(69,173,168)","rgb(84,36,55)","rgb(217,91,67)"]);

var legendText = ["Cities Lived", "States Lived", "States Visited", "Nada"];

//Create SVG element and append map to the SVG
var svg = d3.select("body")
           .append("svg")
           .attr("width", width)
           .attr("height", height);

// Append Div for tooltip to SVG
var div = d3.select("body")
           .append("div")
          .attr("class", "tooltip")
          .style("opacity", 0);

// Load in my states data!
d3.csv("data/stateslived.csv", function(data) {
color.domain([0,1,2,3]); // setting the range of the input data

// Load GeoJSON data and merge with states data
d3.json("data/us-states.json", function(json) {

// Loop through each state data value in the .csv file
for (var i = 0; i < data.length; i++) {

    // Grab State Name
    var dataState = data[i].state;

    // Grab data value
    var dataValue = data[i].visited;
```

```
// Find the corresponding state inside the GeoJSON
for (var j = 0; j < json.features.length; j++) {
    var jsonState = json.features[j].properties.name;

    if (dataState == jsonState) {

    // Copy the data value into the JSON
    json.features[j].properties.visited = dataValue;

                // Stop looking through the JSON
                break;
                }
            }
        }

        // Bind the data to the SVG and create one path per GeoJSON feature
        svg.selectAll("path")
            .data(json.features)
            .enter()
            .append("path")
            .attr("d", path)
            .style("stroke", "#fff")
            .style("stroke-width", "1")
            .style("fill", function(d) {

            // Get data value
            var value = d.properties.visited;

            if (value) {
            //If value exists...
            return color(value);
            } else {
            //If value is undefined...
            return "rgb(213,222,217)";
            }
        });


        // Map the cities I have lived in!
        d3.csv("data/cities-lived.csv", function(data) {

        svg.selectAll("circle")
            .data(data)
            .enter()
            .append("circle")
            .attr("cx", function(d) {
                return projection([d.lon, d.lat])[0];
            })
```

```
        .attr("cy", function(d) {
            return projection([d.lon, d.lat])[1];
        })
        .attr("r", function(d) {
            return Math.sqrt(d.years) * 4;
        })
            .style("fill", "rgb(217,91,67)")
            .style("opacity", 0.85)

    // Modification of custom tooltip code provided by Malcolm Maclean, "D3 Tips and Tricks"
    // http://www.d3noob.org/2013/01/adding-tooltips-to-d3js-graph.html
    .on("mouseover", function(d) {
    div.transition()
            .duration(200)
        .style("opacity", .9);
        div.text(d.place)
        .style("left", (d3.event.pageX) + "px")
        .style("top", (d3.event.pageY - 28) + "px");
    })

    // fade out tooltip on mouse out
    .on("mouseout", function(d) {
        div.transition()
            .duration(500)
            .style("opacity", 0);
    });
});

// Modified Legend Code from Mike Bostock: http://bl.ocks.org/mbostock/3888852
var legend = d3.select("body").append("svg")
                    .attr("class", "legend")
                .attr("width", 140)
                .attr("height", 200)
                    .selectAll("g")
                    .data(color.domain().slice().reverse())
                    .enter()
                    .append("g")
                .attr("transform", function(d, i) { return "translate(0," + i * 20 + ")"; });

    legend.append("rect")
        .attr("width", 18)
        .attr("height", 18)
        .style("fill", color);
    legend.append("text")
        .data(legendText)
        .attr("x", 24)
        .attr("y", 9)
        .attr("dy", ".35em")
        .text(function(d) { return d; });
    });
});
</script>
</body>
</html>
```

TWO CASE STUDIES

Reading about others' experiences when creating a visualization is helpful because we see the thought processes and decision making behind the design. Here are two students' experiences as they think through an InfoVis problem: Shayne Murray's "Stereotype as Reality" and Bonnie Gardner's "Where Does UNICEF Collect Data?"

Case Study 1: Shayne Murray's "Stereotype as Reality"

Visualization: https://public.tableau.com/profile/shayne.murray#!/vizhome/profile OfAnAmericanShooter/Dashboard1?publish=yes

Who Am I?

My name is Shayne Murray (figure 5.19) and I am a second-semester student at Simmons University in Boston, Massachusetts. My desire to take Professor Beno-ît's Information Visualization course stemmed from my previous experience with technology courses at Simmons. During my first semester I took LIS 488, Technology for Information Professionals, which is required for all LIS students. I enjoyed the class immensely, and decided to continue learning about different aspects of technology during the rest of my time at Simmons. Professor Benoît's course was the perfect fit in terms of challenging my technological abilities and forcing me to look at things through a graphic design lens.

FIGURE 5.19 Shayne Muller. *Shayne Muller*

Software

For my project, I used the data analytics and visualization software Tableau. The software's "click-and-viz" capability made connecting to the data (Excel format) extremely easy, and my limited programming and graphic design background was no hindrance, as Tableau has many easy-to-learn tools for first-time users in order to create appealing data visualizations.

Who Is the Audience and Why Is a Computer-Based Visualization Necessary?

Unfortunately, American mass shootings are becoming more and more common with each passing year. With this being the case, the creation of visualizations that focus on different aspects of mass shootings will be increasingly important. Computer-based visualizations are needed because they communicate data more effectively than other methods. While my visualization, as compared to others throughout the web, is elementary, other fact-based visualizations will be needed in order to educate our nation, hopefully resulting in meaningful gun control legislation and the allocation of national resources toward mental health care.

Design Decisions

Because of space limitations I chose a pie graph for the race category, metaphorical symbols for the sex category, and a basic chart with symbols for the mental illness category. Although data visualization experts such as Edward Tufte advise against using pie charts when creating visualizations, I chose it due to its ability to capture the audience's attention and quickly orient the viewer to the material. I believe the symbols I used for both the sex and mental health categories also create a clear and precise way for the audience to understand what's going on. To separate the various aspects of the visualization, I focused on font color and strength to divide them. Red was the most obvious choice for the focal point of the visualization because of its ability to capture attention while signaling a sense of danger. The headlines for each section are black in order to separate them from the rest of the descriptive text. For fonts, I switched from two presets from Tableau: book and medium. I found them clear to read, and I didn't want to include flashy text that would take away from the focus of the visualization. I layered the percentage text over the graphics for the first two visualizations because it helped alleviate the space constraints, and also made for a more appealing visualization.

Data

The qualitative data I used for the field headings were race, sex, and mental health status. Race was composed of various data fields including White, Latino, Black,

Asian, Native American, and a category labeled "other." Sex was a binary field (male and female), and mental health status consisted of yes (a history of mental illness confirmed), no (a history of mental illness was not confirmed), unclear (contradictory information), and unknown (the shooter's mental health status was not publicly available). These four categories made up the qualitative elements of the dataset, while the quantitative measurements consisted of a sum of all the shooters from 1982 to 2017.

Because *Mother Jones* did such extensive reporting on the three data types (gender, race, and mental health status) for the American mass shooters, it wasn't necessary for me to do any data cleaning. In a perfect world, it would be great to add further character attributes such as level of academic attainment, marital status, employment, and so on to better flesh out the identity of the mass shooter, and persuade my audience that resources should be diverted to education, job training, mental health, and other social programs that have been suffering in recent years.

Roadblocks

I sacrificed function when layering the percentages associated with each category. In the ethnicity visualization, the percentage box hovers over some parts of the pie chart, making it either hard to see each slice of the pie or making it impossible to hover over the slice of the pie and further examine the field values. I don't think this lessened the impact of the visualization because I wanted the audience to be able to understand the information at face value, regardless of whether the visualization worked properly.

Bibliography

Berinato, S. (2016, June). Visualizations that really work. *Harvard Business Review.* Retrieved from: https://eds-a-ebscohost-com.ezproxy.simmons.edu /eds/pdfviewer/pdfviewer?vid=3&sid=22431029-463f-4c1d-a618-9202739 d3cb7@sessionmgr4006

Swann, A. (1987). *How to understand and use design layout.* Cincinnati, OH: North Light Books.

Tufte, E. R. (1990). *Envisioning information.* Cheshire, CT: Graphics Press.

Zappaterra, Y. (2007). *Art direction + editorial design.* New York, NY: Abram Studios.

Case Study 2: Bonnie Gardner's "Where Does UNICEF Collect Data?"

Visualization: http://web.simmons.edu/~gardneb/lis473/d3demos/d3/Final_Project/

Introduction

I am an MLIS graduate student at Simmons College (figure 5.20), and my programming background started two years ago when I took a mandatory technology course for my program. We learned HTML, CSS, and some JavaScript, and I was hooked. I immediately changed my program focus to information science and technology, and I've been expanding my programming skills ever since. I have taken an introductory course in Python, a data interoperability course, and most recently an information visualization course. I was inspired to learn about information visualization because I hope to utilize such skills in the humanitarian/NGO (nongovernmental organization) sector doing information management and analysis.

FIGURE 5.20 Bonnie Gardner.
Bonnie Gardner

My Project

Originally, I had planned to use United Nations (UN) data to make a parallel coordinates graph where each country would be a line and each axis would represent different country statistics. However, I soon realized that the data was not collected consistently enough to be used in this way. There was a significant difference in the number of countries used in each dataset, which got me wondering which countries were being used, and why. I changed my visualization to explore this question.

My visualization is a world choropleth that depicts the location and frequency of data collection by the United Nations Children's Fund (UNICEF). (See figure 5.21.) Each country is color-coded based on how often it is included in datasets—the darker the color, the more frequently it is used. The view can also be filtered by categories of data. It uses data from the UN's open access data repository and focuses specifically on UNICEF data. It is meant to be an exploratory visualization that highlights trends of current UNICEF data-collection practices as well as possible gaps in information availability.

The Design

This choropleth is created using d3.geomaps, and the design details are largely dictated by the d3.geomap library, which formats the choropleth for you. Because I was using UN data, I chose to try and keep the aesthetic qualities as close to UN standards as possible. For the color scale, I used nine shades of blue to represent the UN and to display sufficient variation in the data. I also used an official UN font, Avenir, for the page's title and description. The background color is Ancient White to better contrast with the blue and to make the filter form more noticeable. I placed the filter form in the upper-left corner so as to be easily visible and readily understood that there was interactivity in the visualization. This visualization is not designed for the general public. It is meant for researchers or humanitarian professionals. The visualization, although fairly simple in form, represents complex data that requires a familiarity with the data, or at least with humanitarian aid and/or global politics, to analyze effectively.

The Data

The data was sourced from the UN's data repository at http://data.un.org, where the organization gives open access to all of their datasets and allows these to be downloaded in multiple formats. Within their vast collection of datasets, they have a folder titled "The State of the World's Children," which is a list of datasets collected by UNICEF. For this visualization, I downloaded all 116 datasets in CSV format and stored them in a folder on my computer. I wrote a Python program to walk through every file in the folder, open the file, pull out the first column containing the country names in string form, convert them into a list, and write that list as a row in a master CSV file. The result was a CSV file with each row representing a UN dataset and consisting of all of the countries used in that set. I then separated the UN files into category folders and performed the same program, resulting in a CSV file for each category. I used a second Python program to count how many times each country was used per category in integer form.

A d3.geomap requires a CSV file to be used and also requires a country Unit ID. I used the three-letter country codes defined in the ISO 3166-1 Alpha 3. I pulled the country codes from a Wikipedia page (https://en.wikipedia.org/wiki/ISO_3166-1_alpha-3) and put them into their own CSV file. I had to edit the country names in the country ID CSV file to match the UN's country naming format. I wrote a Python program to collect the country IDs into a list and then went through all of the category lists and added the number count for each. I used the Pandas Python library to convert these lists into a data frame and wrote it to a CSV file where the rows were the countries and the columns were the categories. The visualization uses a ratio scale based on the number of datasets for each country and, although the data is in integer form, a d3.geomap converts the legend to float form as default.

Data Analysis

To separate the datasets into categories, I had to decide how broad or narrow I wanted the analysis to be. To go broad could eliminate some more nuanced revelations, but going too narrow could result in a limited number of datasets for comparison. I eventually decided to go with a narrow categorization. I felt that showing views with greater specificity would more effectively highlight any data collection focuses or gaps. Categories included: Total, Births, Children, Deaths, Education, Economy, Healthcare, Health, and Population. There were a couple of other initial categories that were eliminated due to too few datasets in the category. For example, literacy was a category that only had three datasets, therefore, for the purposes of this visualization, I chose to include literacy in education. An important aspect of the categories is that they are not distinct. A dataset could be included in more than one category. They are not meant to be parts of a whole, but instead layers of overlapping components.

The category titled Total is obviously the total list of datasets. The Births category involved data directly related to the act of giving birth, as well as the support immediately following the birth. The Children category involved data pertaining specifically to children and did not include the adult population. The Deaths category includes data on the number and the causes of deaths. The Education category included data on education, literacy, and learning. The Economy category includes data on wealth distribution and use, both at the government level and the individual or family level. The Healthcare category included data that specifically involved healthcare professionals or healthcare coverage. The Health category involved the general health and wellness of the population. The Population category involved data on the number of living people.

Computing

The technology used for this visualization includes d3.js, especially d3.geomaps, and Python. These allow for interactivity in the visualization. The form in the top left lets you change views by selecting different category data from which the map is colored. You can also zoom in on the map by clicking on a country and zoom out by clicking on white space. If you hover over a country, you also get a tool tip that lists the name of the country and the number of datasets for that country.

Outcome

Overall, I am happy with how the project concluded. However, with more time I would like to add a bar graph beneath the choropleth that depicts the number of datasets per category. I also think that this project could be easily scaled to include the entirety of the UN data repository and could be updated in real time using the website's application program interface (API). In addition, I would like to add to the tool tip to include a list of the datasets for that country and link out to the actual data. In order to accomplish this, I would need a different way to process the data and it was suggested from the audience that I consider an object-oriented approach, which I will explore.

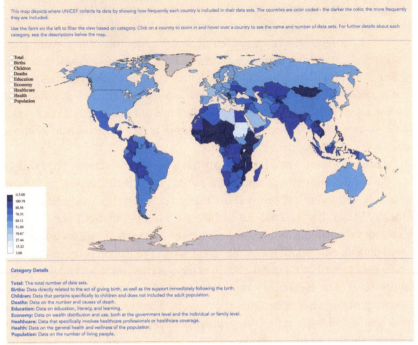

FIGURE 5.21 Where Does UNICEF Collect Data? *Bonnie Gardner*

References

ColorBrewer2.0. (n.d.). Color advice for cartography. Retrieved from http://color brewer2.org/#type=sequential&scheme=BuGn&n=3

d3.geomap. (n.d.). Choropleth Map: World. Retrieved from https://d3-geomap .github.io/map/choropleth/world/

ISO 3166-1 alpha-3. (n.d.). Wikipedia. Retrieved from https://en.wikipedia.org /wiki/ISO_3166-1_alpha-3

United Nations. (n.d.). Guidelines on the use of the UN emblem. Retrieved from https://outreach.un.org/mun/content/guidelines-use-un-emblem

United Nations. (n.d.). UN Data. Retrieved from http://data.un.org/Explorer .aspx?d=UNESCO

CONCLUSION

Constructing visualizations is an iterative process. We might accidentally focus too narrowly on one part of the whole—the data, the user, the interactivity, the graphic design—and fail to see the whole. A communications-oriented approach places the end user in the fore, to be sure, with the information visualization creator commanding multiple modes of expression to lead to a truthful interpretation of the data and enable cognitive engagement to establish meaning and to learn unexpected trends from the data.

REFERENCES

See also the trend in incorporating the end user in iterative design and info services: IS-EUD: International Symposium on End-User Development.

Arnheim, R. (1969). *Visual thinking*. Berkeley: University of California Press.

Arnheim, R. (1974). *Art and visual perception*. Berkeley: University of California Press.

Arnheim, R. (1982). *The power of the center: A study of composition in the visual arts*. Berkeley: University of California Press.

Börner, K. (2014). *Atlas of knowledge*. Cambridge, MA: MIT Press.

Börner, K. (2016). *Atlas of science*. Cambridge, MA: MIT Press.

Burkhard, R. A., Andrienko, G., et al. (2007). Visualization summit 2007: Ten research goals for 2010. *Information visualization, 6*(3), 169–188.

Drucker, J. (2014). *Graphesis: Visual forms of knowledge production*. Cambridge, MA: Harvard University Press.

Eagleton, T. (1991). *The ideology of the aesthetic*. New York, NY: Wiley-Blackwell.

Heer, J., Viégas, F. B., & Wattenberg, M. (2007). Voyagers and voyeurs: Supporting asynchronous collaborative information visualization. *CHI 2007 Proceedings—Distributed Interaction*, pp. 1029–1038.

Jacomy, M., Venturini, T., Heymann, S., & Bastian, M. (2014, June 10). ForceAtlas2, a continuous graphing layout algorithm network visualization designed for the Gephi software. *PLOS.* https://doi.org/10.1371/journal.pone.0098679

Meirelles, I. (2013). *Design for information*. Beverly, MA: Rockport.

Moghaddam, B., Tian, Q., Lesh, N., Shen, C., & Huang, T. S. (2004). Visualization and user-modeling for browsing personal photo libraries. *International Journal of Computer Vision, 56*(1-2), 109–130.

Munzner, T. (2014). *Visual analysis and design*. London: CRC Press.

Pousman, Z., Stasko, J., & Mateas, M. (2007, November-December). Casual information visualization: Depictions of data in everyday life. *IEEE Transactions on Visualization and Computer Graphics, 13*(6), 1145–1152.

Steele, J., & Illinsky, N. (Eds). (2010). *Beautiful visualization: Looking at data through the eyes of experts.* Sebastopol, CA: O'Reilly.

Tufte, E. R. (1990). *Envisioning information*. Cheshire, CT: Graphics Press.

Ware, C. (2008). *Visual Thinking for Design*. Burlington, MA: Morgan Kaufman.

## CHAPTER 6

The Data of Visualization

We reviewed the computing architecture of visualization (the client-server model), an increased list of visual shapes (our visual semantics), composition (the syntax, as it were), and how interactivity with the end user emulates human-human communication. Engaging the viewers' minds in an internal and external conversation is to engage the inquisitive mind and begin the transformation of data to meaningful information, or the pragmatics of visualization.

For this topic we consider the data themselves and how web-based interactivity responds to the growing volume, variability, and values of the data we wish to use.

The outcomes bridge the realm of computer technology and the people who need and who will use the visualizations. There is a knowledge gap between programmers, end users, data providers, and information professionals that, if not considered, will block real understanding of the challenges to creating and using visualizations. As data science courses become popular among students and researchers, information professionals should be there to fulfill a vital technology-user role, both guiding and creating new information resources.

We review a use case scenario of working in an office or research setting to model exporting data from common tools (Excel, Access, SQL, PHP, Python) and take the steps needed to prepare the data for visualizations. Along the way, a variety of examples of increasing detail are grafted to the original model, leading to a more holistic process.

BUILDING BLOCKS

Not unlike any systematic investigation, the major building blocks of visualization start with a few rules. In these notes, we look at some main ideas—to provide an overview of themes so that you can see how wide-ranging the topics are and hone in on topics of particular interest. Use these lengthy points (based on Börner's [2016] and Duarte's [2008] works) as a way of integrating our readings, design labs, and software experiences into a methodic approach in order to be sure to cover all the bases. Note that while certain themes dominate, there are many different workflow approaches when progressing from datasets to a final product.

Conceptual Frameworks: Use Case Scenarios

Many frameworks from various disciplines, among them the sociology of science, scientometrics, infometrics, operational research on science, and the diffusion of knowledge, are applied to data and information visualization studies. So for new students of visualization, it can be daunting to try to recall all the required steps. However, by detailing questions to ask, it is possible to be more certain of covering important specifics and actions when creating the visualization, as well as to create your own checklist.

Units

Of primary importance is understanding the data. If you have taken a statistics course, you might think of data as being nominal, ordinal, interval, or ratio. These concepts translate into computer languages in different ways. Nominal (or categorical) data are represented computationally through strings. A string is a contiguous chain of characters (e.g., var name = "Matt Damon"). Ordinal and interval data can be of any computer data type—*integer* (int, or counting numbers, 1234), *float* (or floating point, 1.234), *double* (usually very long numbers, such as 1.2345678987e300). Ratio data, too, can be of any numeric type. Other important types are Date (05/17/2018, or in the ISO standard of YYYY/MM/DD, e.g., 2018/05/17) and boolean (true/false, 0/1).

- *Data units.* In your data files, are the units of data single units? groups? or various independent groups linked to form larger aggregates? For instance, is the first pass at categorizing the data based on a boolean value (e.g., all respondents who answered "true"), or by a nominal/string value such as Group 1, Group 2, and so on?
- *Basic, aggregate units, and linkage.* As part of cleaning and preparing the data, you may need to work not with basic units such as a raw value, but rather some derived values. Note that in practice, databases and other data stores might not contain values that can be calculated. A paycheck amount

is aggregate data, a value calculated from operations on other fields, such as hourly_wage * hours_worked. When using these data, either calculate and store the aggregate data or include functions in your scripts to calculate them.

- *Specifics of the data.* Are they alphanumeric (A–Z, 0–9), integers, floating point numbers, categorical/nominal (strings), binary (true/false, 0/1), or characters and bytes? Some of the aggregate data may be statistical—indeed, a key component of visualization is establishing trends and doing so based on statistics. Tables 6.1 and 6.2 introduce a comparison of statistical terms and their computer programming equivalent. The second table suggests what types of statistical techniques are likely to be applicable. A course or two in statistics, particularly regression, covers these points more fully.

TABLE 6.1	
Comparison of terms between statistical work and programming equivalents	
Statistical term	**Sample programming term**
Interval scale (positive or negative values)	Floating point; integer (positive values only)
Ratio scale	Floating point
Counting numbers (usually non-negative)	Integer
Binary data (e.g., m/f, pre-test/post-test group)	Boolean
Categorical data (such as blood type A, B, O; work groups [admin, finance, training]; playing card suits (hearts, spades, diamonds, clubs)	Enumerated type (aka "factor" in R programming language)
Random vector	List or array (e.g., myData = [1, 2, 3, 4]; tuple, dictionary in Python; array in JavaScript, PHP)
Random matrix	Two-dimensional array; .json file structure
Random tree	Tree; .xml file structure (parent-child relationships and nodes)

TABLE 6.2
Conversion chart and statistical tests

Data type	Possible values	Example usage	Level of measurement	Distribution	Scale of relative differences	Permissible statistics	Regression analysis
Binary	0, 1 (arbitrary labels)	Binary outcome ("yes/no", "true/false", "success/failure", etc.)	Nominal scale	Bernoulli	Incomparable	Mode, Chi-squared	Logistic, probit
Categorical	1, 2, ..., K (arbitrary labels)	Categorical outcome (specific blood type, political party, word, etc.)		Categorical			Multinomial logit, multinomial probit
Ordinal	Integer or real number (arbitrary scale)	Relative score, significant only for creating a ranking	Ordinal scale	Categorical	Relative comparison		Ordinal regression (ordered logit, ordered probit)
Binomial	0, 1, ..., N	Number of successes (e.g. yes votes) out of N possible	Interval scale	Binomial, beta-binomial, etc.	Additive	Mean, median, mode, standard deviation, correlation	Binomial regression (logistic, probit)
Count	Non-negative integers (0, 1, ...)	Number of items (telephone calls, people, molecules, births, deaths, etc.) in given interval/area/volume	Ratio scale	Poisson, negative binomial, etc.	Multiplicative	All statistics permitted for interval scales plus the following: geometric mean, harmonic mean, coefficient of variation	Poisson, negative binomial regression
Real-valued additive	Real number	Temperature, relative distance, location parameter, etc. (or approximately, anything not varying over a large scale)	Interval scale	Normal, etc. (usually symmetric about the mean)	Additive	Mean, median, mode, standard deviation, correlation	Standard linear regression
Real-valued multiplicative	Positive real number	Price, income, size, scale parameter, etc. (especially when varying over a large scale)	Ratio scale	Log-normal, gamma, exponential, etc. (usually a skewed distribution)	Multiplicative	All statistics permitted for interval scales plus the following: geometric mean, harmonic mean, coefficient of variation	Generalized linear model with logarithmic link

From https://en.wikipedia.org/wiki/Statistical_data_type

Data Acquisition and Preprocessing

Is your data gathering complete? Document the source of the data file(s). Are the data preprocessed completely—no null values, data are comparable, publicly available large datasets?

- Data acquisition: 80 percent of time spent on a project is data acquisition and preprocessing. Many research visualization projects employ very large datasets. It's typical to use freely available collections from institutions or on the Internet. Indeed, about 50 percent of biomedical literature is free from the U.S. National Library of Medicine (NLM); other large datasets for researchers are available from universities. Moreover, most cities, states and provinces, and national governments and international agencies offer publicly accessible datasets.
- Dataset types: Can you classify the dataset into an immediately recognizable category? Time data, for example, may not need to be measured down to the microsecond, but you can recognize it as a time measurement. Once identified as "time," you can select choices for analysis, modeling, and layout with more confidence.
  - *Time.* Are the units measured usefully by days, months, years; seconds, microseconds, or Coordinated Uniform Time (UTC; https://www.time anddate.com/worldclock/timezone/utc)? These types are particularly important: date (in YYYY-MM-DD format), date-time (YYYY-MM-DD HH:MI:SS), time stamp (e.g., 2018-09-07 00:00:01' UTC), and year (YYYY).
  - *Geography.* If the data are primarily geographic, do they represent physical geography? Do they represent a basic image of the landscape, over which some other data trends are presented, such as migration? In this case, consider using an SVG map below the interactive visualization. See Syracuse University Libraries' helpful research guide on geographic data (https://researchguides.library.syr.edu/c.php?g=258118&p=1723814).
  - *Topics or concepts.* Subject discipline lists extracted from library files are a first source of large datasets in LIS. Topical data can be from any source and of any type, but in libraries and archives, they may reflect subject tracings, user-provided terms, or other controlled vocabularies and ontologies; these are useful for suggesting related ideas.
  - *Full-text documents.* If your work uses full text documents, such as a corpora of some work or some author, there will be a lot of data to process. Consequently, the visualization may become rather complex, too. Ask how the relationships between the texts will be defined and how to link the related themes that emerge. Here, force-graph and arc techniques are popular.

o *Raw data from scientific research.* As with full text, presenting raw scientific data requires careful preparation of the data. A common mistake is to convert the scientific data, often represented by a float or double, to a smaller number form, an integer. In this case, the precision of the data is lost (e.g., 3.14159 becomes just 3).

Data Analysis, Modeling, and Layout

Here is where the original layouts, wireframes, experience decomposing, and analyzing others' visualizations come into play. Having classified the data to be shown, what type of visual patterns are best for your model? What specific data facets should you include? These decisions will impact both the choice of interactivity and the choice of color pallet. Should your visualization include density of a single value, or will you choose a color gradient or discrete color units to represent the change?

- From simple to complex: Do the data based on the attribute values represent a trend from a lower value to a higher one (e.g., the number of times so-and-so tweets or a phrase appears in a journal or discipline)?
- Temporal pattern matching (TPM): A temporal pattern is a smaller unit of a larger pattern, such as a melody from a song. Another example is a children's growth chart for an entire classroom; we may wish to identify growth patterns of a subset of the children. Time patterns are very popular in machine learning, such as evaluating television watching habits, or assessing highway traffic flow patterns (e.g., Diggle, 2013) (figures 6.1 and 6.2).
- Geographic features (area, surfaces, density, and boundaries): Geographic feature maps certainly are popular. This kind of chart relies on the viewers' ability to recognize landmasses. The map of Los Angeles (figure 6.3) applies a monochromatic scale from lowest to highest density. The population cartogram (figure 6.4) manipulates the actual geographic dimensions of these European Union countries using a complementary color scheme. In neither case do the colors have any intrinsic significance other than visual clarity.
- Semantic properties (dimensionality reduction and clustering): Mapping semantic properties can be a wonderful challenge because the data vary greatly at the semantic level, which in turn affects the clustering possibilities. The semantic model chart (figure 6.5) combines a spreadsheet-type list of the source data and then a force-directed graph identifying the domain ontology, number of classes and properties, and source. The designer opts for less data, more clarity, and relies on the end users scrolling to the source to see more relationships. Conversely, figure 6.6 demonstrates a much greater volume of data (and how volume impacts design choices). In this chart the data are clustered into concepts, represented by the colored bubbles, and within each bubble subgroups are identified using icons (the triangles, the size of which suggests word density). Finally links (or edges) demonstrate other types of relationships between the larger bubbles and individual data points (or words).

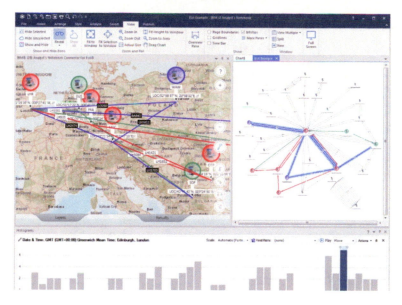

FIGURE 6.1 Temporal and geospacing data: three chart techniques representing the same data. *https://www.ibm.com/us-en/marketplace/analysts-notebook*

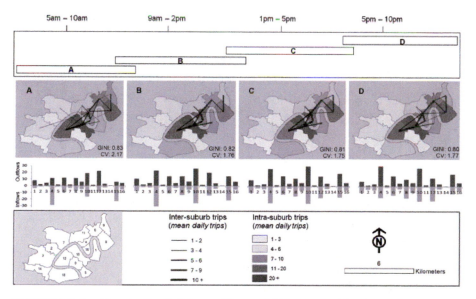

FIGURE 6.2 Another geospatial map with several keys to explain the green map and bar graph's relationships.

FIGURE 6.3 Geospatial map building on user's familiarity with the LA Basin, supplemented with local landmarks—highways, cities, and color key for density of the data. *https://www.epa.gov/smartgrowth/smart-location-mapping*

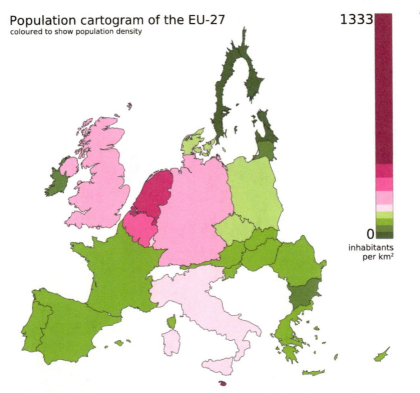

FIGURE 6.4 Manipulating the familiar physical map of Europe based on population data. *Public domain; https://commons.wikipedia.org/wiki /File:EU-_Pop2008_1024.PNG*

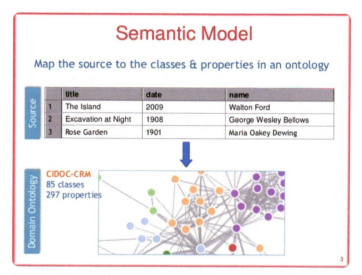

FIGURE 6.5 Here both raw data source and representation are presented. The force-directed graph on the bottom is not intuitively explanatory. The viewer "reads" the raw data to interpret the unlabeled visual version.

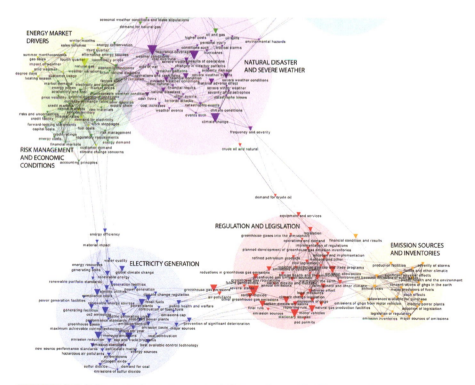

FIGURE 6.6 When confronting a lot of data, color, arcs, labels, and icons disambiguate set memberships and provide a rich "text" for the viewer to "read." Sustained engagement with an interactive visualization yields much greater understanding of potential meanings and application.

Network features (density, degree centrality, reachability): See figures 6.7 and 6.8.

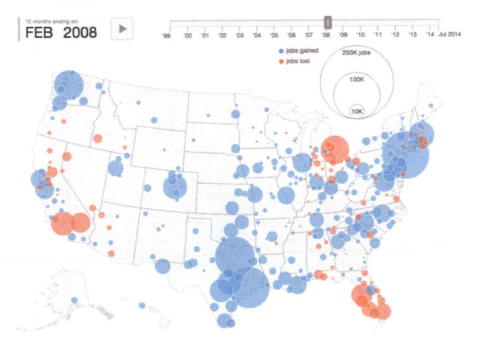

FIGURE 6.7 This map relies on a neutral gray background map (to situate the viewer), then two complementary colors for clustering the groups, a key for suggesting the data values, and finally a slider to allow the viewer to interact with the data. *AxisMaps*

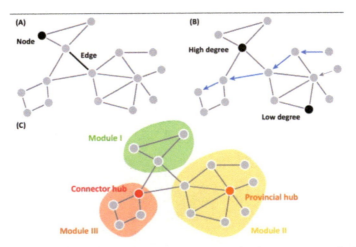

FIGURE 6.8 In these force-directed graphs, the use of color and arrows facilitates identifying clusters. *Courtesy of the author*

Models: Descriptive and Process

A model links to the viewers' engagement with the visualization. Can the viewers identify the purpose and create a relationship in their mind between the nascent message of your visualization and their knowledge and work practices? When sketching out the design and considering the data, what is the first intention of the design? How will viewers interpret the goal of the visualization? These are the main approaches:

- Descriptive: The descriptive process is primarily the domain of information graphics, but of course any visualization first describes a phenomenon. Such graphics are usually static, such as a number chart, spreadsheet, newspaper graphic, article citation counts, networks of citations, composition of knowledge domains, or new research themes extracted from journals.
- Persuasive: Having worked in litigation graphics, I learned that the visual expressions of data help explain complex concepts to juries. Graphics can in subtle ways persuade more than convince a jury. In contemporary InfoVis, there is the ethical commitment to truthfulness. We can still try to persuade, provided the viewers can access the raw data and interact with them (Pandley, Manivannan, Nov, Satterthwaite, & Bertini, 2014; Hullman, 2018).
- Explanatory: Does the visualization explain a phenomenon? The idea of explaining suggests a conversation. To that end, then, the visualization needs to keep the end user engaged through design (typography differences for type of content, such as headlines, labels, statistical data, content text; color differences of degree; interactivity). Explanatory visualization enables the viewer to see *why* something happened in addition to *what* happened.
- Exploratory: Can the viewer learn more than the obvious and explanatory planes? Being able to *explore* the data necessitates interactivity, communication, and data. Think of such exploration of data as "what if" scenarios, through which the viewer learns what she or he did not know. This exploration leads to what I term "candidate meanings" because such signification makes sense to the end user but has not yet been tested in real life.
- Process models (aka predictive models): Some researchers and obviously some data types do not include the predictive part of visualization, partly because the popular statistical regression techniques in data visualization describe a limited time frame and can be unreliable for future events. Instead the predictive strength is partially intuition. The viewer might predict in a mixed qualitative/quantitative way likely trends by incorporating domain knowledge, experience of the phenomenon, and a host of other unenumerated factors. There is also a computational reason. Clustering of data can introduce a degree of statistical error. Computationally, relying on intuition is reduced by increasingly large and varied datasets which are

subjected to myriad artificial intelligence and machine learning techniques. For more on machine learning, see appendix B.

- *Data Layout*: The spatial layout of datasets is the storytelling. Like any good story we follow the tale, identify with the characters, and should apply the lesson!

Data Communication

Figure 6.9 suggests steps in the process of acquiring and processing data, role of analysis and modeling, and the steps in realizing the visualization. It is a kind of "life cycle of creating visualizations." The chart is a bit complex, so I'll comment on each numbered point. Following this discussion, there is a use case study set in an office or research office to consider when implementing an InfoVis service.

Visualization layers as a systematic guide to building the visualization. To help cover all the bases, reflect on the design from each of the numbered layers in the figure. For example, the layout (the design and guides, such as scales, grids, or the "reference system") serves as the base level of the visualization. Next, consider whether the reference layer's guides are being interpreted as part of the visualization's message (which they are not) or as part of the reference frame.

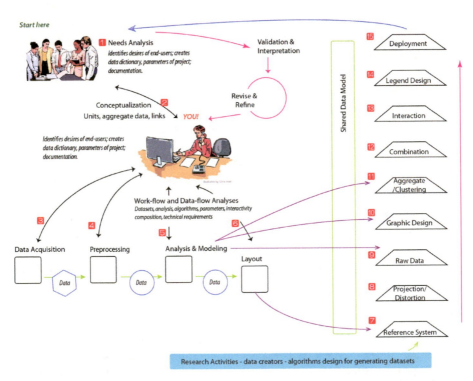

FIGURE 6.9 An office-work view of the InfoVis process. *Courtesy of the author*

- Needs analysis (step 1). This activity is a usual starting point in all projects. As part of the larger world of systems analysis, needs analysis (or needs assessment) activities elicit what the clients/patrons believe they need, determine interface features, and identify data sources and create documents, such as data dictionaries, necessary for understanding data sources. Likewise, we convert what we learn from the patrons into a "logical model" of the new work flows and data processes that lead to new "physical models" of the new computer systems. (Read more about this on the companion site.)
- Steps 1 and 2 are mutually informing. As you identify the client needs, conceptualization by the specialist (2) applies the questions listed earlier in this chapter as part of the fuller documentation of the project. Discuss the design with people on your team; consider testing the message by presenting the design to a pilot group, and then survey their opinions. There will always be variation, but are their opinions mostly the same?
- Data acquisition (3) can be as basic as extracting data from a relational database of library or archival records, or as complex as integrating large collections of text, raw scientific data, and research data. Whatever the resources, it is important to identify the sources. This includes file names and types or URLs, a "dictionary" identifying the data types and examples, and identifying restrictions on the data. Medical data, for example, have a number of protective restrictions.
- Preprocessing (4) includes data cleaning.
- Analysis and modeling (5) may or may not occur at this point. Some researchers or patrons may do their own data cleaning, derivative data creation, and statistical analysis. The fields of data analysis, machine learning, and data science generally are areas of expertise requiring considerable math, computing, and statistical skills.
- The layout component (6) is the initial design of the graphic where you consider the aesthetics of the design, tempered by the type of data to be displayed.
- Reference system (7) refers to creating visual/graphic clues in the design that help the viewer frame the image for interpretation. For example, without any clues, people tend to read as they read text: from top left to bottom right. By adding a reference system in a neutral gray color, viewers chunk the parts of the design and identify their function in the overall design. The eye tends to ignore the reference system once an interpretive framework has been established by the viewer's mind. Including a visually dominant clue, as we see in a bubble chart or in a directed graph, viewers will break from reading the model to locating another way to read the graph. A force-directed graph or other kind of parent-child relationship could be directed to read from a central node (or "centroid"). See figures 6.10 and 6.11.

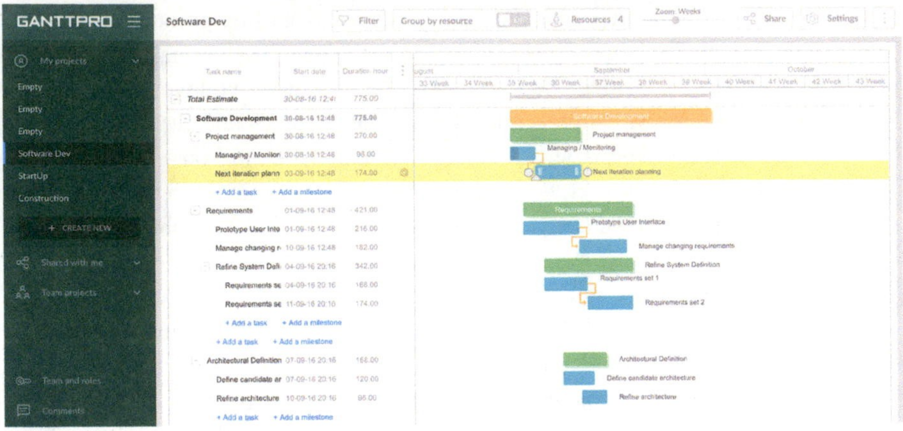

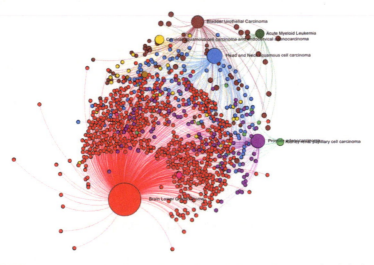

FIGURE 6.10 Gantt charts help manage resources, but interactive visualizations of a project facilitate understanding the living nature of work. *Ganttpro.com*

FIGURE 6.11 A more complex force-directed graph that relies on color, labels, and colored arcs to clarify relationships of the subgroups and their relationship with each other.

- Projection/distortion (8) refers to adjustments to the image, either to emphasize some aspect of the data (such as the European population distortion map) or to add more room for other parts of the graph to be emphasized (Kosara & Hauser, 2003).
- As an issue of transparency, trust building for the viewer, and to conform to many grant-funded project requirements, the raw data of a research project

should be available to viewers (9). The data may be available through a link, a common technique, or as a major part of the visualization (as in the semantic example described above).

- The graphic design (10) of the visualization at this point should be informed by a more intimate knowledge of the data, along with the user needs and experience. Finalize layout composition, color theme, typography, and the functional blocks of texts or subgroups in the design.
- Aggregation and clustering (11) are part of data preparation and analysis. When the dataset is very large or varied, it is usual practice to cluster the data into manageable groups. For instance, instead of posting a large number of individual values or subjects, cluster the data into groups, not unlike a contingency table.
- For combination (12), we can adjust the overall design and issues associated with integrating the data, the balance of data and aesthetics, and which data to interact with viewers.
- Interaction (13) moves the combined aesthetics + data into the communications realm of the visualization. To achieve the interaction layer, we revisit the d3 JavaScript to ensure that the designed interactive events work as

Example using a slider to change the data values and the response in color transparency

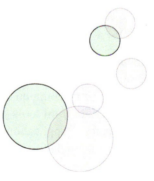

Records per bubble

Records per bubble

20

82

FIGURE 6.12 Provide sliders or other responsive techniques so end users can adjust the volume of data to be shown. In this example, the numeric value of the slider is used to recalculate the color density. *Courtesy of the author*

needed. For example, a mouse-over event can trigger a <div> tag to show the underlying raw data source. For time-space series data, it is useful to include a slider so that end users can investigate the progress of the changes. At each change in the slider, the script updates the color on the screen. (See figure 6.12.) As an example, say in a bubble chart, the color transparency reflects the volume of the data in the bubble. Values < 10 might be rgba(128, 128, 128, .1). As the slider advances to the midpoint, the script updates the alpha channel to reflect the change: rgba(128, 128, 128, .5), until the maximum value is reached: rgba(128, 128, 128, 1). As InfoVis has become more common and complex, the layout of the designs tends toward a composite layout, with the functional regions discussed above. Consequently, it is useful to group all the interactive controls into a "control panel" to accept user input and display the recalculated values.

- Finally, having iterated the legend design and data for a penultimate potential visualization (14), label the graphics and controls in ways that direct the users' "reading" of the graphic.
- (15) Deploy! Test your visualization with a pilot study and update.

Design Lab

On the companion website, there is a detailed lab applying the specifics of the above steps to a visualization project of library research journals.

A HOW-TO GUIDE—CASE STUDY

Throughout the text, we've emphasized the *thought* behind creating interactive information visualizations. We've looked at the tech and the data of visualizations. Demonstrating some common office practices is helpful. We first need to examine how to export data from tools you use on the job—spreadsheets (such as Excel, Numbers), database applications (such as MS Access, MySQL), and other applications—into shareable file types. Text files are the most convenient and reliable way to share data across computer platforms and applications. These include plain text (.txt), text files with tabs and new lines to preserve records (usually .csv, comma-separated values, and .tsv, tab-separated values) and semi-structured text files, .xml and .json.

Use Case Scenario

In this scenario, a research office has been collecting data using spreadsheets. Each researcher has his or her own spreadsheet with the same fields. Ostensibly the researchers collect the same types and fields of data, but not the same values in the fields. At the end of the project the data are reviewed prior to (a) performing any statistical tests, (b) calculating (or deriving) new fields from the data, (c) clustering and classifying data for the project and for computer processing in general, and, of course, (d) visualization.

Scenario: Data Exported from a Spreadsheet/Spreadsheets

The various spreadsheets are exported to the new text file as "tab-delimited." This means the individual fields in a row of data are separated by a tab character (\t) and each row is terminated by a "new line" character (\n) (table 6.3). Depending on the software, such as Excel, the file can be named .tsv (e.g., researchGroup1 .tsv; table 6.4). Common text file endings including .dat (for data), .txt (for text), .csv (comma-separated values), .tsv (tab-separated values). Recall that .json and .xml have a structure to the data that must be applied correctly, else the file cannot be used. Tab-separated value files are the most forgiving . . . unless you miss a tab!

In this scenario, the individual files have all been integrated into a single .tsv file.

TABLE 6.3
Structure of exported tab-delimited data

	field_1	\t	field_2	\t	field_3	\t	...		field_x	\n
row_1										
row_2										
...										
row_y										

TABLE 6.4
Structure of exported tab-delimited data with column names, row names, and data

	Name	Delimiter	Age	Delimiter	Phone	New line
record_1	Tom	\t	22	\t	5123	\n
record_2	Jane	\t	29	\t	3392	\n
record_y Maria		\t	32	\t	9922	\n

Creating a text file by hand for hundreds or millions of data points would not be efficient, nor would it be easy to check for errors or to update the data. Consequently, most of us use spreadsheet applications or a relational database (RDBMS) product, such as Access, MySQL, or Oracle. Creating shared data stores is easy, but checking the health of the data and transforming raw data to a model that can be communicated visually with others can be an impediment.

Scenario: Data Ingested from Spreadsheets into SQL

It is not uncommon for projects to be merged. Imagine digital library collections from a number of library departments being integrated into a single institutional repository. Once data have been exported to a .csv or other text file, a single SQL command (MySQL, 2018) can import all or only selected fields from the .csv to a table. We need the name of the source .csv, the name of the database table, the delimiter (e.g., a comma), and how each record is terminated (the \n). In the following coding example is a command to ingest data in a Unix terminal window from the file called HealthData.csv to a database table called 2018HealthCare and stored in fields named "idno," "disease," and "protocol":

> load data local infile 'HealthData.csv' into table 2018HealthCare fields terminated by ',' enclosed by "" lines terminated by '\n' (idno,disease,protocol)

This is only an example—your version of SQL and your platform requirements may differ. The main point is to know that there are file options and that these are within your skill set. It's important to know the file manipulation possibilities. The file contains 271,351 records, each having 21 fields, for a total of 5,698,371 individual data points. The first line of the output details the names of each of the fields in the original file:

> ind_id,ind_definition,reportyear,race_eth_code,race_eth_name,geotype, geotypevalue,geoname,county_name,county_fips,region_name,region_ code,license_type,numerator,denominator,percent,ll_95ci,ul_95ci,se,rse, ca_decile,ca_rr,version

Clearly, trying to type such a long data file by hand into a new file is unreasonable and fraught with likely errors. A knowledge of how to export/import data from/to different file formats is vital (see table 6.5). Even if your job does not employ these skills, being aware of solutions that can be executed in-house or in your department is usually the most feasible, immediate path toward agility and responsiveness as information services evolve.

TABLE 6.5							
Exporting data from various file types to other types							
source →	export to	source →	export to	source →	export to	source →	export to
.csv	.txt .tsv .csv .xml .json	.tsv	relational database tables	txt	.xml .json	.xml	.json

To emphasize that librarians and other information specialists can and should be active participants in creating and deploying new services, specifically information visualization, there are several scripts provided to facilitate data conversions. These scripts and the full-fledged program you can use are available on the companion website.

Looking at data sources in a general way shows how data reside in various "silos." For instance, a library staff who sponsor several digital library projects may decide ultimately to share data from across these collections. Some resources may be in relational databases or be MARC (machine-readable cataloging) records; other projects may be already in an .xml instantiation, such as visual resources association (VRA4), extended archival descriptors (ead), and others; some files may have some or no structure. In figure 6.13 we see a variety of data options and several programming/scripting tools common in LIS, namely PHP, Python, Java, and perl. Once the data have been ingested and prepared, they may be output to other containers, for other projects, and streamed to the end users' interfaces. Understanding the technical infrastructure and data sharing techniques allows us to explore and to improve services.

An office-oriented work process: export your data, clean them, output new files, and stream to visualization software.

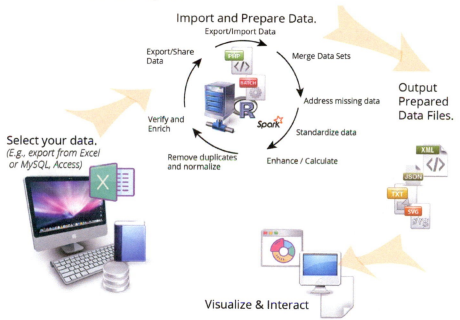

FIGURE 6.13 Presenting architectures for data and visualization work share the same computing technologies and work behaviors but often reference different user-oriented descriptions. Here the emphasis is on providing terms for activities already commonly performed on the job. *Courtesy of the author*

CONVERTING DATA FOR SHARING AND VISUALIZATION

Consider now the cleaning of the data. If there are null values or cells with no values, you must decide how to address this. In survey research, if the number of respondents (*n*) is large enough, then incomplete records may be dropped from the project. Other projects may need to have some value stored in the missing field. There are several techniques; we cannot delve deeply into them here. One technique is to store a very small number (if the field contains numeric values), such as 0.03, to introduce an identifiable level of noise in the data. Adding such a value prevents accident multiplication or division by zero or throwing an error message, such as NaN (not a number) or NULL value.

To ingest these into your database, first export the contents as a .csv, tab-delimited, or xml file. From .xml there are applications, or you can easily write a script to convert the .xml file to a .json file.

Options? Here are demonstrated scripts to convert from different formats, as well as an example of an online converting utility, Code Beautify (https://code beautify.org/; figure 6.14).

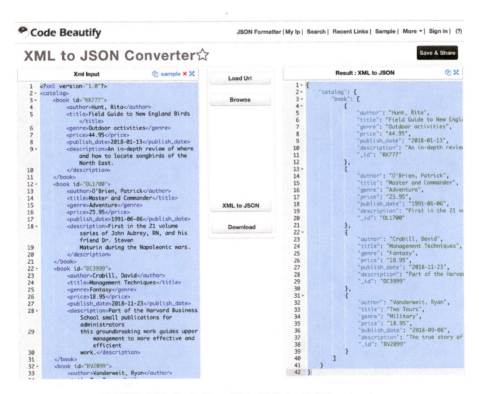

FIGURE 6.14 Code Beautify's XML to JSON converter.

Knowing the names of the fields and the format of the data, we can combine heterogeneous data sources into a single common file format. There are many techniques for combining and mapping between datasets. Some techniques are called "cross-walks" (Zhang & Chen, 2006); other techniques include creating an enterprise-wide XML schema to integrate conceptually similar fields while preserving the original semantic tags (Benoît, 2016) or individually querying RDBMS tables and ingesting the data into a single source, a data warehouse.

CLEANING THE DATA

Before progressing to analysis and visualization of the data, examine the data for inconsistencies and missing values. Data that fall outside an expected range, values that are missing or null, or have a different encoding or data type need to be addressed. Salary data is a good example. An hourly student worker wage might be between $10.00 and $17.50 an hour; the number of hours worked each week might be between 0 and 40 hours. Data for the pay rate would need to be checked (it is possible for someone to accidentally enter $100/hour or even .10/hour) as well as the hours worked (no value less than 0, no value greater than 40).

Sometimes data from multiple sources, or an inconsistently created single source, may represent the same idea, but the actual content of the fields cannot be easily compared. A medical subject heading (MeSH) for adenosine triphosphate (ATP, an organic chemical in the body that is used in intercellular energy transfer and is a precursor to DNA and RNA) is expressible by the MeSH Heading (Adenosine Triphosphate), tree numbers (D03.633.100.759.646.138.236 or D13.695.667.138.236 or D13.695.826.068.236), or one of 19 entry terms, or preferably by its unique ID: D000255 (National Library of Medicine, 2018). This means that inconsistent data must be "mapped" from one to the other. Numeric values create their own important challenges. When combining integer data with other forms, such as long, double, or float, the data could lose precision if "cast" to the wrong format. The integers (counting numbers, 1, 2, 3, etc.) are not as precise as the other types, such as a "float" that is used to express numbers with decimal points, e.g., 3.14159. Casting a float to an integer reduces π to just 3. Such a loss of precision would be a disaster!

Missing values can be addressed based on the data and your task. In a research project, if there are a large number of responses, the researcher may choose to delete records that are not complete without negatively affecting the statistical power of her work. In some situations, however, it may be better to introduce a certain level of "numeric noise" in the data as described earlier, such as filling empty cells with a tiny value (e.g., 0.03), or comparing the same cells and determining some average value that could be inserted in the empty cells. The researcher knows the data are skewed, but is able to adjust accordingly in the project.

Finally, among the many things we should check is the zero value. Of course, any multiplication by zero returns a zero. Accidentally allowing this value to go unchecked displays wildly inaccurate values.

Once the dataset is cleaned, it is ready either for analysis or presentation. d3 and Tableau have tools to read entire sets of data from these file types, and we can do the same with a PHP script. The script can be run in a terminal window or integrated into a web server for real-time processing.

CONVERTING A TEXT FILE TO .XML OR .JSON

Once the data are exported from a spreadsheet or another text file, it is useful to convert the data from a text file to an .xml or a .json file. As noted above, sometimes multiple files must be integrated. In these examples of a PHP script, a .tsv file is read and processed with the results being stored in a new .xml file. Another example creates an .json file from multiple text files. Notice that we can use "factories" such as XMLFactory, and some programming languages (Java) and other languages have readers and writers that facilitate processing .xml and .json (e.g., PHP's XMLWriter() class and its json_encode() method). d3.js has a function for easy importing of .csv/.tsv, .xml, and .json file formats.

Demo 1: .tsv to .xml (tsvToXml.php)

For this example, the PHP script is run directly from the terminal window. By default, there is a hard-coded source file (demo.tsv) and a hard-coded target or output file name (demooutput.xml). First identify the xml tags to be used, and map them to the field names in the input file. This demonstration script can be run as a stand-alone program using your terminal window or on a web server, using an html <form method="post" action="tsvToXml.php"> command.

The resulting output file looks like this (but with actual data):

```
<?xml version="1.0">
        <data>
                <refnumber>
                <location>
                <name>
                <age>
                <other>
        ...
```

```php
<?php
echo "\n\n\t\t*** Processing files ***\n\n\n";
$lineNo = 1;
$xmlWriter = new XMLWriter();
$xmlWriter->openUri('demooutput.xml');
$xmlWriter->setIndent(true);
$xmlWriter->startDocument('1.0', 'UTF-8');
$xmlWriter->startElement('root');
$tsvFile = new SplFileObject('demo.tsv');
$tsvFile->setFlags(SplFileObject::READ_CSV);
$tsvFile->setCsvControl("\t");
foreach ($tsvFile as $line => $row) {
    if ($line > 0) {
        echo "\nProcessing $lineNo: \t$row[0]\t$row[1]\t$row[2]\t$row[3]\t$row[4]";
        $xmlWriter->startElement('data');
        $xmlWriter->writeElement('refnumber', $row[0]);
        $xmlWriter->writeElement('location', $row[1]);
        $xmlWriter->writeElement('name', $row[2]);
        $xmlWriter->writeElement('age', $row[3]);
        $xmlWriter->writeElement('other', $row[4]);
        $xmlWriter->endElement();
        $lineNo++;
    }
}
$xmlWriter->endElement();
$xmlWriter->endDocument();
echo "\n\n\t\t*** File done. ***\n\n\n";
?>
```

Demo 2: .tsv to .json (tsvToJson.php)

This script demonstrates integrating several .txt files in the same folder and outputting a single .json file. Here we also apply a regular expression (regex) that looks for any tab, space, or comma and "cleans" them out. The variable $clean is actually an array; each member of the array (e.g., $clean[0]) is copied to a more useful variable (such as $userName = $clean[2]). The variables named zero, one, two, three, and so on are there to underscore the correspondence between the source file's field position and where they are in the outputted .json file. In real practice these names should be changed to reflect the actual contents so that people reading the file can follow the work.

```php
<?php
$people = [];
// Grab all the .txt files
foreach (glob('*.txt') as $filename) {
    echo "\n\t\t*** Processing $filename ***";
    $handle = fopen($filename, 'r');
    if ( $handle ) {
        // run line by line through the files
        while (( $line = fgets($handle) ) !== false) {
            // grab the fields
            echo "\n\tProcessing Line: ".$line;
            $clean = preg_split("/[\s,]+/", $line);

            // e.g., what the fields are in the tsv file
            // 200   Jones    Mary  22    6.5    BMW  0    441-4321
        // All the fields in the input file(s)

            $zero = $clean[0];
            $oneAndTwo = $clean[1]." ".$clean[2];
            $three = $clean[3];
            $four = $clean[4];
            $five = $clean[5];
            $six = $clean[6];
            $seven = $clean[7];

            $people[] = [
                'field 0' => $zero,
                'field 1 and 2' => $oneAndTwo,
                'field 3' => $three,
                'field 4' => $four,
                'field 5' => $five,
                'field 6' => $six,
                'field 7' => $seven
            ];
        }
        print_r($people);
        // write to json file
        $jsonwrite = fopen('people.json', 'w');
        fwrite($jsonwrite, json_encode($people));
        fclose($jsonwrite);
        fclose($handle);
    } else {
        echo "Sorry, cannot open the file";
    }
}
echo "\n\t\t ***** File Done. ****\n\n";
?>
```

In Gardner's UNICEF case study discussed in chapter 5, her Python approach seems to be a typical encounter when adopting open data sources. These data are not often cleaned or consistent, requiring the visualization specialist to analyze the data and then programmatically prepare the data for graphing.

In her use case description in chapter 5, Gardner describes the preparation of the data:

> The Data: The data was sourced from the UN's data repository at http://data .un.org, where the organization gives open access to all of their datasets and allows these to be downloaded in multiple formats. Within their vast collection of datasets, they have a folder titled "The State of the World's Children," which is a list of datasets collected by UNICEF. For this visualization, I downloaded all 116 data sets in CSV format and stored them in a folder on my computer. I wrote a Python program to walk through every file in the folder, open the file, pull out the first column containing the country names in string form, convert them into a list, and write that list as a row in a master CSV file. The result was a CSV file with each row representing a UN dataset and consisting of all of the countries used in that set. I then separated the UN files into category folders and performed the same program, resulting in a CSV file for each category. I used a second Python program to count how many times each country was used per category in integer form.
>
> A d3.geomap requires a CSV file to be used and also requires a country Unit ID. I used the three-letter country codes defined in the ISO 3166-1 Alpha 3. I pulled the country codes from a Wikipedia page (https://en.wikipedia.org/wiki /ISO_3166-1_alpha-3) and put them into their own CSV file. I had to edit the country names in the country ID CSV file to match the UN's country naming format. I wrote a Python program to collect the country IDs into a list and then went through all of the category lists and added the number count for each. I used the Pandas Python library to convert these lists into a data frame and wrote it to a CSV file where the rows were the countries and the columns were the categories. The visualization uses a ratio scale based on the number of datasets for each country and, although the data is in integer form, a d3.geomap converts the legend to float form as default.

Here are the Python scripts (countCountries.py and getCountryData.py) she wrote for these data from http://data.un.org/Explorer.aspx?d=UNESCO. As a student in a library and information science program, her work demonstrates the suitability of LIS students and professionals participating in creating InfoVis services. Live examples appear in the companion website. (Note that the code is not optimized; it seems the programmer opted for clarity and repetition of similar functions for legibility for neophytes.)

file name: getCountryData.py

```
# file name:  getCountryData.py
# Author: Bonnie Gardner, Spring 2018 InfoVis class.
# I downloaded all of the UNICEF data files into a folder in CSV format
# This program walks through all of those files, Removes the first column (country names)
# and writes them as rows into a new csv file.
# The source files are from  http://data.un.org/Explorer.aspx?d=UNESCO


import csv
import os
import glob


myData = [] #create a list of lists; each list item is a list of countries

# Give the file path of the folder you want to walk through
# The below path is -hard-coded-.  Replace with your own data source file path or URL
path = "/Users/bonniegardner/Desktop/Viz Data/Total"

# for each file in the folder, open the file, read it, separate it into lines
# and store them in a variable (fileLines)

for file in glob.glob(os.path.join(path, '*.csv')):
    countries = []  #make a list to store the country names
    readFile = open(file,'r')
    fileLines = readFile.readlines()
    readFile.close()

    # for every line, pull out the first column (country name) and add it to the countries list
    for l in fileLines:
        data = l.split(",")   #split lines into an array based on columns
        country = data[0]  #the first column is the name of the country
        countries.append(country)     #add the country name to the list of countries
    myData.append(countries)          #add the list of country names to the master list of lists

# write myData to a new csv file, with each list of countries as a row in the csv file
with open("totalData.csv", "w") as c:
    writer = csv.writer(c)
    writer.writerows(myData)
c.close()
```

```
# Results is a csv file with rows containing a list of countries for each file in the folder
# Run for each category folder
# end of the script
```

```python
# file name:  countCountries.py
# Author: Bonnie Gardner, Spring 2018 InfoVis class.
# This program reads the country data csv files from each category folder,
# It counts the number of times each country is included and writes the result
# to a master csv file.

import csv
import pandas as pd
from collections import OrderedDict

# create dictionaries to count the countries. Key = country name, Value = count
total = {}
births = {}
children = {}
deaths = {}
education = {}
gov_Econ = {}
health = {}
healthcare = {}
population = {}
country_ID = {}

# create a structured list to later turn into csv rows
rows = []

# List of dictionaries
dict_List = [total,births,children,deaths,education,gov_Econ,health,healthcare,population]

#For each category, create a dictionary and count the countries
def total_count():
readFiles = open("totalData.csv", "r")      # open file
    fileLines = readFiles.readlines()         # separate into lines and store in variable
    readFiles.close()                         # close file
```

```python
        # for each line
        for l in fileLines:
            data = l.split(",")                  # split into an array of country names
            for d in data:                       # for every country name
                d = d.replace('"', ")            # remove extra quotation marks
                if d not in Total.keys():        # if the country name not already in the dictionary
                    Total[d] = 1                 # add to the dict; set count by 1
                else:                            # if the country name is in the dictionary
                    Total[d] += 1                # increase the count by 1

    """for k in Total:
        print(k, Total[k])
    """


def countTheDataa(listName, fileToRead):              # births_count():
    readFiles = open(fileToRead, "r")
    fileLines = readFiles.readlines()
    readFiles.close()

    for l in fileLines:
        data = l.split(",")
        for d in data:
            d = d.replace('"', ")
            if d not in listToRead.keys():
                listToRead.keys[d] = 1
            else:
                listToRead.keys[d] += 1

            """ for k in listName:
            print(k, listName[k])
            births_count()
            """


# create and structure the rows
# uses a file (CountryIDs.csv) that contains the country IDs for each country
def make_rows():
    readCSV = open("CountryIDs.csv", "r")   # read Country ID file
    CSVlines = readCSV.readlines()          # separate into lines and store as variable
    readCSV.close()                         # close file
```

```
for l in CSVlines:                          # for each line in the Country ID file
    lines = l.split(",")                    # split into array based on columns
    country = lines[1].strip('\n')          # country name is second column; strip the extra \n
    ID = lines[0].strip('\ufeff')           # country ID is the first column; strip the extra
    if country in Total.keys():             # If the country name is included in the Total dict keys
        list = [ID]                         # create a list with first value as the country's ID
        for dict in dict_List:              # for each dictionary in the dictionary list
            if country in dict.keys():      # if the country name is included in that dict's keys
                x = dict[country]           # add the count from that country to the list
            else:                           # if the country name is not in that dictionary's keys
                x = "NaN"                   # add the value "NaN" to the list, if an empty value
            list.append(x)                  # Creates a list containing the country's ID
                                            # and the counts for each category
        rows.append(list)                   # add the list to the list of rows
return(rows)

# pandas creates a data frame for the master csv file
# first indicate the data for the rows, then name the columns
# write the data frame to the master csv file
def make_CSV_file():
    df = pd.DataFrame(rows, columns=["Country_ID", "Total", "Births", "Children", "Deaths",
"Education", "Gov_Econ", "Healthcare", "Health", "Population"])
    df.to_csv('UNdata.csv')

# now that the functions are defined for each area, call them to prepare data and create files.
for counts in dict_List:
health_count()
healthcare_count()
gov_econ_count()
education_count()
deaths_count()
child_count()
total_count()
births_count()
make_rows()
make_CSV_file()
# end of the script
```

REVIEW

This topic reading included many streams of approach as we progress from thinking about information graphics and some design principles to understanding and practicing data capture and transformation to shared formats. The information visualization designer must have both the big picture and the smaller technical focus in order to

- work with the end-user in determining the needs;
- explore the data sources and determine what sources (RDBMS, .xml, .txt, .csv, .tsv, .json) and fields are to be included;
- clean the data and create the "data warehouse";
- cover the basis for what models can be applied to process the data, to analyze the data;
- know what questions to ask to ensure that all aspects of the data + design have been reviewed;
- follow the visual and interactive leads suggested by the data type and the model (e.g., geospatial data + time series model);
- have sufficient hands-on skills to convert data, to gain a sense of "ownership" of the data and analyses;
- reflect on fast-paced trends in visualization and vocabulary—from a client-server architecture to the idea of "information ecologies," touching on complete integrated systems (such as Hadoop) and how vocabularies created by designers, computer scientists, or end users usually conflict but can reflect the same concepts (e.g., "ecologies" as a holistic view of systems);
- be able to leave a trail back to the original data, metadata, and other resources that help end users and the designers trust the data—a key function of explaining and exploring data and avoiding persuading without facts.

QUESTIONS AND PRACTICE

- On paper, sketch out the "technical infrastructure" of an information visualization system (build off the client-server model) so that you can integrate PHP scripts to process data.
- Practice applying PHP scripts to processing .tsv files and exporting them as .json and as .xml files.
- Practice d3.js just to import the files you've created; check the browser's console for the resulting array.
- Review your data and make decisions how you might cluster/aggregate the data. Important questions:

o What kinds of error might you introduce into the data?

o Can you balance the loss of precision of the data and the aggregation?

o How will your client and your consumers of the data know about the source data and your statistical analysis?

o Consider the role of your candidate layouts/designs/models. Could you lead a discussion with clients to test the potential visualization?

• As an option (and a very important one), extract what we have reviewed about layout, aesthetics, and graphic design, along with the review questions above, and create a manual that you could use to "train the client."

Clustering and Classification

Large datasets are usually clustered. The reason for the clustering depends on the project. For example, if we collected data about American political movements, we could cluster first into Democrat and Republicans. Then within each group we may subdivide into wings (Tea Party, Conservative, Liberal, and so on). The level of granularity of our clusters stops at the subdivision. The rest of the data provides information about movement specifics.

Clustering also reduces the amount of computer resources that must be dedicated to processing at one time. It is more efficient to execute an algorithm on a subset of data instead of on an entire data collection. Imagine how long it would take to sort data into alphabetical order if there are millions or even billions of data points! Clustering also helps us to determine the starting point of our visualizations. For instance, say we have 14 subclusters from two groups. Each of the subclusters exhibits some relationship between each member. Using the political party example, we might want to see who ran against whom, or among the parties, which candidates have the highest ranking on political opinions, based on some common standard. Consequently, we might think of a bubble graph: Each candidate represented by a circle (bubble); the two main parties represented by their own color. Color shading could indicate the degree of left- or right-leaning. Then drawing the edges (lines) between each of the bubbles might be based on some criterion that interests us, such as voting history on a controversial issue.

Given the current American political iconography, the colors of blue and red are automatically in play as choices (https://en.wikipedia.org/wiki/Red_states_and_blue_states). But to create the "political feeling" of a graphic, as live reporting does, an InfoVis can consider the popular icons of elephant and donkey, as well as other political iconography in the data display. Although this approach may feel better suited for a poster or static information graphic, the inclusion of familiar iconography and live data harmonizes streams of public information.

New programmers sometimes struggle with the balance of computational efficiency versus human understanding of the data and of the code. Unless one is working with extremely large data sets, it is better to err on the side of people. Through the interaction of others with our data, as well as our own questioning and learning, the InfoVis we create will become both humanly and computationally more easily interpreted and used. For instance, it is better to document the data and the coding/scripts such that people who will maintain and update your code and data in the future can easily interpret your code rather than to try to write computing code that looks very dense, thinking it will be executed more rapidly. As various kinds of information professionals integrate interactive InfoVis services, it is clearly optimal to understand and deliver reliable services than to deflect patron requests.

REFERENCES

Benoît, G. (2016). Metadata for information discovery. *Journal of Library Metadata, 11*(3-4), 129–154.

Börner, K. (2016). *Atlas of knowledge*. Cambridge, MA: MIT Press.

Chan, L. M. & Zeng, M. L. (2006, June). Metadata interoperability and standardization—a study of methodology part I. *D-Lib Magazine, 12*(6). Available from http://dlib.org/dlib/june06/chan/06chan.html

Diggle, P. J. (2013). *Statistical analysis of spatial and spatio-temporal point patterns* (3rd ed.). New York, NY: CRC.

Duarte, N. (2008). *Slide:ology*. Sebastopol, CA: O'Reilly.

Hullman, J., Drucker, S., et al. (2013). A deeper understanding of sequence in narrative visualization. *IEEE Transactions on Vis. Comput. Graph., 19*, 2406–415.

Kosara, R., & Hauser, H. (2003). An interaction view on information visualization. *Eurographics 2003*. Retrieved from https://cdn.mprog.nl/dataviz/excerpts/w5/Kosara_Interaction_View.pdf

MySQL. (2018). 13.2.6 Load Data Infile Syntax. Retrieved from https://dev.mysql.com/doc/refman/5.7/en/load-data.html

National Library of Medicine. (2018). Adenosine triphosphate. MeSH Descriptor Data 2018. Retrieved from https://meshb.nlm.nih.gov/record/ui?ui=D000255

Pandley, A. V., Manivannan, M., Nov, O., Satterthwaite, M. L., & Bertini, E. (2014). The persuasive power of data visualization. *New York University Public Law and Legal Theory Working Papers*, 474. Retrieved from http://lsr.nellco.org/nyu_plltwp/474

## CHAPTER 7

Real-World Visualizations and Text Visualizations

Introducing visualizations with data that are familiar to the target audience encourages engagement and discussion. Given the dominance of humanities-educated librarians, this section introduces text-oriented visualizations and visualization of ontologies.

Popular interest in InfoVis seems to have evolved rapidly in the public eye, first through video dashboards. As anecdotal evidence, we see these colorful charts at the airport, in businesses, in colleges announcing events, stats, and even in weather reports. Press outlets publish articles about the need to visualize (Hartnett, 2015); Northeastern University offers a master of fine arts degree in "information design." The increase in student and researcher use of visualizations, particularly in digital scholarship, has led to numerous inquiries into what software to use to create one's own visualizations. Academic libraries have responded by providing helpful guidelines. Integrating InfoVis of any kind into any organization should be carefully planned. For example, purchasing a software product that is unknown to the staff and technology staff requires training; if the infrastructure of an organization does not yet permit easy extraction and reshaping of data, then there is another layer of work to be added. Moreover, if the staff do not know about their data, or know how to prepare and share data, then more costs can be incurred.

A logical response is to provide updated computer skills so that staff members can understand their own data and use existing and a few new related skills. For instance, several large international corporations have stalled projects because there was neither knowledge or technical channels for data to be shared; when the files were available to the staff, they did not know how to convert from one format to another (in many cases, how to convert data to a tab-delimited text file) (Benoît & Hussey, 2011; Benoît & Agarwal, 2012). Or, management purchased an information system that claimed to be able to share data with existing systems, when in fact, it became necessary to retain an outside consulting firm to convert the data, purchase new systems and applications, and hire programmers. Basic computer-use skills today require everyone to know how to convert data, to export data in various formats, and be willing to share data. The shift in baseline technical skills reminds one of the introduction of word processing and the job title of "word processing specialist" in the 1980s. Today, of course, every job requires word processing.

Moreover, charts/graphs and interactive visualizations are expected in student papers and research reports. Harvard College will start to require all undergraduates to take a data science course, just as the students are required to complete a foreign language, English, and math courses. Consequently, institutional infrastructure, and educational and library services must respond by offering new services and support.

Another take on this phenomenon is the communication of science and of knowledge. Creating a stand-alone visualization both serves student needs for their work and creates a new digital resource shared with other information seekers through the library.

WHAT SHOULD YOU KNOW?

Contemporary information specialists should at least be conversant in the pros/cons, benefits and liabilities, tech and data requirements of each software product they might use. In-house professional development courses provide opportunities to create (and to learn from failures), as does an environmental scan of software products as part of typical professional practice, similar to keeping up on publishing as a collection development librarian would. (A list of products appears in the appendix B and in the online companion site.)

The hands-on technical skills of today's professional are far-reaching. Having reviewed 1,000 entry-level positions in academic and research libraries (2015–2017), it appears that 30–40 percent of these positions required or preferred applicants with skills in

- HTML5;
- CSS;
- JavaScript;
- Various file types (.csv, .tsv, .xml, and .json formats);
- PHP (or other scripting or programming language, such as Java or Python);
- Structured query language (SQL; MySQL, Oracle).

From this list and through experiences consulting with companies (Benoît & Hussey, 2011) we suggest that the positions require hands-on skills with the structure and presentation of data, along with skills to store, retrieve, and integrate data. The consequential next step seems to be expanding the programming/scripting component to include Python, the most popular programming language in data science; the d3.js libraries that build on knowledge of HTML, CSS, and XML (and various implementations, such as SVG); and experience reading and writing from/to files of different formats; specifically:

- Searching and outputting data from SQL to .csv, .tsv, .xml, and .json formats
- Selecting and reducing datasets from one file type (such as .csv) to another (such as .tsv or .json)
- Running and/or writing Python and PHP scripts to output data to an appropriate data format (e.g., from a large open source data store such as data .gov)

To achieve these ends, as part of professional and staff development an institution can offer updated training in computing, information system architectures, data interoperability, scripting/programming, and structured query language. These technical skills require contextualization, or the *why* of the new services, such as "how information visualization can benefit our patrons and services."

CASE STUDY: HARVARD UNIVERSITY LIBRARIES

C. M. Boyd, Research Data Management Program, Harvard University

Ceilyn Boyd. *Ceilyn Boyd*

Building Workflows for Everyday Visualization

Background

As a program manager for the Harvard Libraries I am called on to collect and analyze data related to my projects and initiatives, develop data-informed recommendations, and communicate results to our stakeholders. I regularly use ad hoc data visualization to support these activities.

Programs with well-defined services and users, and widely agreed upon performance metrics, might use data dashboards to aggregate and visualize operational statistics. However, not all organizational contexts are quite so neat. Building a data dashboard may not be practical for programs that must respond to the concerns and requirements of diverse stakeholders, are involved in many projects having diverse or complex data inputs and outputs, or where consensus around performance metrics is lacking.

Resource constraints—particularly time, money, and staff—also affect the ability of a program manager or project team to use data visualization. For instance, a small, four-person team with a tight deadline may not have time or expertise to write custom software to present their results: simple charts generated from a spreadsheet may suffice. Legal, ethical, usability, and sustainability considerations may also impede the ability of a project team to use visualization to explore their data or to share visualized results and data stories. I find that ad hoc data visualization is effective in these circumstances.

The use case below demonstrates a structured, constraint-aware approach I use to quickly design, implement, and document data visualization work flows that are part of larger project or program data life cycles. The approach also recognizes that visualization often occurs at the very end of a complicated data aggregation and analysis work flow.

The Project

The Colonial North America Project (http://colonialnorthamerica.library.harvard .edu) is a large-scale, multiyear effort to digitize all of Harvard University's archival materials dating from 1650 to 1800, totaling over 500,000 manuscript pages from 1,700 collections at 14 of Harvard's libraries. The project was begun in 2012 and is nearing completion. Once complete, Colonial North America will make available thousands of digital objects including digitized letters, account ledgers, ships' logs, diaries, deeds, and birth and death certificates.

During my involvement, the project involved staff from 14 different libraries and archives, and 7 separate departments and groups: archival processing, materials conservation, digital imaging, digital preservation, program management, library information technology, and finance and accounting.

The Need

Of the three common use cases for data visualization—(interactive) data exploration, reporting, and data storytelling—the Colonial North America project primarily required lightweight, minimalistic visualization for reports on project performance characteristics. During a later phase of the project, I was able to create more elaborate visualizations to provide a richer picture of the contents of the project manuscripts.

The Data

Prior to the start of digitization, a year-long survey was conducted to identify manuscript materials across Harvard from the Colonial period and pertaining to North America. That data, in combination with a variety of datasets provided by each of the seven departments, was periodically aggregated, combined, and analyzed to measure project progress and productivity, and to inform decisions about resource allocation.

Production information included monthly, quarterly, and annual metrics such as conservation treatment hours; the number of collections having undergone archival processing; the number of digital images created per month; and the number of digital objects that were deposited in the digital preservation infrastructure and made available to researchers for use via a persistent universal resource name (URN).

The datasets were primarily tabular, but did not exhibit much overlap in reporting categories and time intervals between the departments. Additional descriptive XML metadata associated with manuscript collections and items supplemented the production-related datasets.

The Approach

During the initial phases of the project, there was little standardization of data contributions from each of the departments. Over time, as reporting expectations settled, it became possible to normalize the data inputs and regularize data aggregation to produce standard reports for stakeholders. Examples of typical reports are shown in figures A through D.

A data dashboard using a tool such as Tableau would have been ideal for this purpose. However, due to resource constraints and limitations on how reports could be shared, a more lightweight approach was needed.

The approach assumes that there are three key work flow categories: data sources, data transformers, and data visualizers. A *data source* provides data for the work flow, such as an API, a database, or program, or a file. Data transformers perform data processing. Examples include filters, spreadsheet formulae, and file format converters. A *data visualizer* presents a graphical representation of results suitable for display on a device, in a document, or in print. These components can be connected to form data visualization work flows.

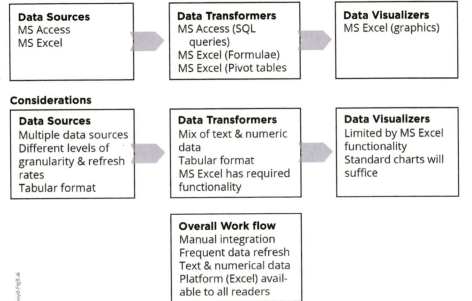

FIGURE A Creating a work flow for integrating a new InfoVis service. *Ceilyn Boyd*

Visualization Work flow with components

Data Sources	Data Transformers	Data Visualizers
MS Access MS Excel	MS Access (SQL queries) MS Excel (Formulae) MS Excel (Pivot tables	MS Excel (graphics)

Considerations

Data Sources	Data Transformers	Data Visualizers
Multiple data sources Different levels of granularity & refresh rates Tabular format	Mix of text & numeric data Tabular format MS Excel has required functionality	Limited by MS Excel functionality Standard charts will suffice

Overall Work flow
Manual integration
Frequent data refresh
Text & numerical data
Platform (Excel) avail-
able to all readers

boyd-Fig B.ai

FIGURE B Visualization work flow: Identifying benefits and liabilities. *Ceilyn Boyd*

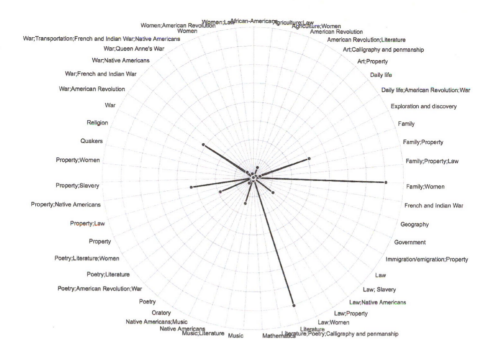

FIGURE C A first plot of identifying subjects from the test visualization collection.
Ceilyn Boyd

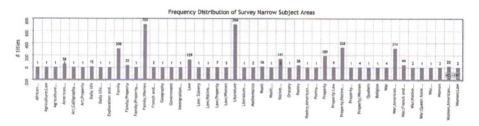

FIGURE D Another representation of the same subject data, plotted in a bar graph.
Ceilyn Boyd

Each of these components has associated dependencies and considerations that should be documented. Work flows may involve legal and ethical, technical, usability, and sustainability considerations. Documenting these considerations makes it possible to maintain existing visualization pipelines and migrate to another visualization platform when needed. Figure C depicts the workflow components and considerations associated with the report shown in Figure A.

Figures D, E, and F are examples of special-purpose visualizations created using combined collections of metadata and project data. The workflow components and considerations shown in Figure G show how differences in visualization purpose and components may affect the types of considerations associated with a workflow.

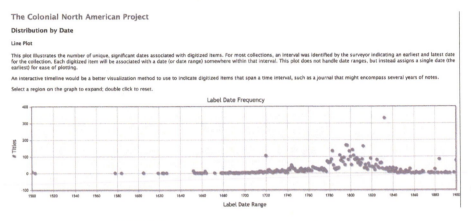

The Colonial North American Project

Distribution by Date

Line Plot

This plot illustrates the number of unique, significant dates associated with digitized items. For most collections, an interval was identified by the surveyor indicating an earliest and latest date for the collection. Each digitized item will be associated with a date (or date range) somewhere within that interval. This plot does not handle date ranges, but instead assigns a single date (the earliest) for ease of plotting.

An interactive timeline would be a better visualization method to use to indicate digitized items that span a time interval, such as a journal that might encompass several years of notes.

Select a region on the graph to expand; double click to reset.

FIGURE E Label data distribution. *Ceilyn Boyd*

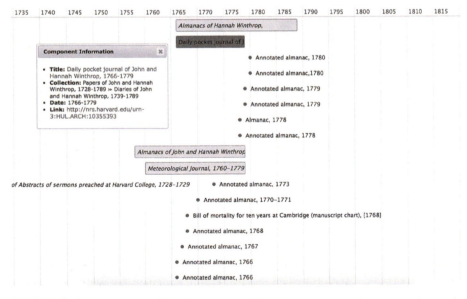

FIGURE F A timeline (not unlike a Gantt chart) with mouse-over details on demand. *Ceilyn Boyd*

Visualization Work flow with components

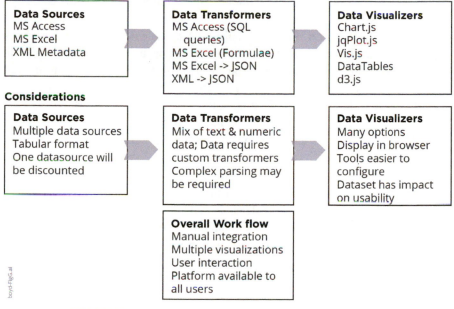

Data Sources	Data Transformers	Data Visualizers
MS Access MS Excel XML Metadata	MS Access (SQL queries) MS Excel (Formulae) MS Excel -> JSON XML -> JSON	Chart.js jqPlot.js Vis.js DataTables d3.js

Considerations

Data Sources	Data Transformers	Data Visualizers
Multiple data sources Tabular format One datasource will be discounted	Mix of text & numeric data; Data requires custom transformers Complex parsing may be required	Many options Display in browser Tools easier to configure Dataset has impact on usability

Overall Work flow
Manual integration
Multiple visualizations
User interaction
Platform available to
all users

boyd-FigG.ai

FIGURE G Updated work processes for InfoVis. *Ceilyn Boyd*

Summary

The visualizations in this example rely on spreadsheets and bar charts for simple reporting, then use custom tools depending on resource availability. Initial challenges, including the heterogeneity of project data and coordinating data streams across different departments, influenced the choice to use simple and readily available data analysis and visualization tools like Microsoft Excel. Over time, as expectations stabilized, it was possible to create custom visualizations of project data. The work flow component method served to document the visualization pipelines to support migration to new platforms as constraints and expectations changed. Ideally, a data dashboard system would be able to span project visualization needs and accommodate different degrees of maturity, data normalization, and stability across a lengthy project life cycle.

ADOPTING THE TECHNOLOGY

A useful approach for introducing new services is to find (or to create) the in-house advocate. In the Harvard Libraries example, the first step in integrating the new service was to demonstrate to the libraries' administration that visualization will help the libraries better understand their services, financial trends, evaluation, and missed opportunities. To this end, the data used in demonstrations were provided by the annual reports of the administration. The resulting product was a composite design of three layers. By recognizing their own data, the part-whole relationships of the institutions' departments, and bolstering confidence in the business intelligence generated by the visualizations by providing access to the source data, the administration immediately saw budget overruns, mismatched patron need/ library service staffing, and technical allocation imbalances among in-house created digital libraries. Just as interesting is the relationship of the visualizations to the libraries' mission. Noting that the libraries were not keeping up with changes in the curriculum exposed a tendency to not use the library as people sought answers elsewhere, departmental and research funds going to purchasing the same tools instead of sharing resources, and interestingly, the loss of "knowledge that leaves the institution when the student leaves or the project ends."

Looking at a slice of probable decision makers in the information professions, Lindquist & Gilman (2008) note that about 68.7 percent of librarians with earned doctorates hold them in the humanities and arts or the social sciences. By using data sources they are likely to be familiar with, such as literature, the arts, and history, we can explore text visualizations and invite their interest in advocating InfoVis services.

Text Visualizations

Text visualizations seem to be a most appropriate introduction point for humanities and literature students. Kucher & Kerren (2015) surveyed 400 different text visualization techniques. This collection suggests a seeming endlessly creative stream of displaying and interacting with text documents, almost all of which will attract an audience, inviting investigation. The range of documents used as source data in the visualizations is notable, too. Many draw from newspapers and literature, but most tend toward sentiment analysis (figures 7.1 and 7.2), automatic topic extraction, and even analyses of the text documents by the visual properties (e.g., font design choices in the original documents; see Brath & Banissi, 2014). Certainly Wordle (Viégas, Wattenberg, & Feinberg, 2009) has taken root in many library and archive homepages.

Other projects about ontologies, related to automatic topic identification, focus more on processing power and data and less on understanding the aesthetics. WebVOWL, for instance, generates visualizations from .json files, created by a Java-based OWL2VOWL converter (Link, Lohmann, Negru, & Wiens, 2018). Evidence of the popularizing of visualization is Ghorbel et al.'s (2016) "Memo Graph: An Ontology Visualization Tool for Everyone," designed "to provide an accessible and understandable user interface that follows the 'design-for-all' philosophy.

FIGURE 7.1 Sentiment analysis project from North Carolina State University, using https://www.jason-davis.com/wordcloud/, a d3 word-cloud algorithm.

FIGURE 7.2 Sentiment analysis with details on demand and radar visualization.

Precisely, it offers an Alzheimer's patient-friendly interface" (p. 265). The point is that there remain technical needs and a lack of attention to the aesthetic—leaving the information professional opportunity to claim the union of arts and sciences in the service of informing people as their own realm.

Word Cloud Generators

A word cloud seems to be a more festive way of presenting a text rather than a particularly effective learning and exploration tool (figure 7.3). Nevertheless, integrating a word cloud on an institution's site is a SOP to adding interactivity and dynamism to a site. There is an opening to add more engagement and more value to the information-seeking session. WordClouds.com's site (https://www.word clouds.com) integrates many of the design questions faced by anyone creating a chart: data source (file or word list), preferred shapes, visual themes, colors, fonts, and distance or gap spaces between visual elements.

FIGURE 7.3 A word cloud demonstrating key terms and the number of those terms by the size of the text. *www.wordclouds.org*

One example is to apply a list of archaic English terms from https://en.oxford dictionaries.com/explore/word-lists/ to the WordClouds.com interactive site. Using the same word list, we can change the composition; applying the South American theme and the same word list yields a different result. Note, though, that the use of archaic English terms as the data do not apply to graphic representing the majority Spanish-Portuguese-French-speaking continent. Nevertheless, moving toward adding visualizations and thinking about the interplay of design and data decisions are a wonderful start.

As a job practice, libraries turn to word clouds as ways of attracting end users, encouraging staff-student participation by creating their own Wordles and supporting visual literacy and metaphor (figure 7.4) (Huisman, Miller, & Trinoskey, 2011). The ACRL/IRIG recently adopted new Visual Literacy Standards, which are described as a "set of abilities that enables an individual to effectively find, interpret, evaluate, use, and create images and visual media" (Huisman, Miller, & Trinoskey, 2011). It is particularly interesting to note that other professional schools—business and law—are actively integrating visualization in the students' toolkit. Harvard Law School (Rios, 2017), for instance, provides links and overviews to online infographics sites, including tag clouds, Gelphi, Dadaviz, Many Eyes, and many others. The reader will notice, though, that many applications easily equate to draining resources for user and technical support and for data conversion.

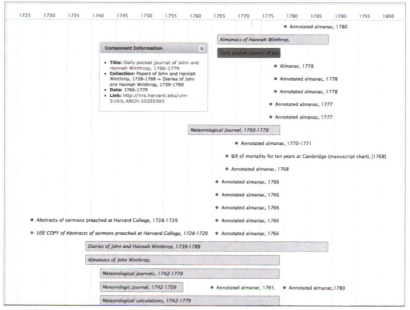

Figure F. Interactive timeline derived from XML metadata for Colonial North America manuscripts associated with John Winthrop, by date. Created using NodeJS and Javascript graphics libraries.

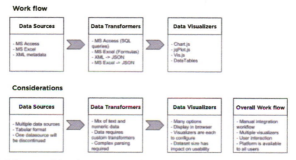

Figure G. Work flow considerations associated with custom data visualizations in Figures D, E, and F.

FIGURE 7.4 Example of an academic library's guide for patrons. *Created by Angela Zoss*

CONCLUSIONS

The use of text-oriented visualizations provides an underexplored opportunity to combine computer technology and human learning experiences, to get more out of the content as well as from the institution's holdings. In the past few years, there has been an uptick in using digital collections—of texts, audiovisual ethnographic documentaries, cultural artifacts—in a text-transcribed form to create a novel, visually intense way of interacting with resources. Stockinger (2015) and Shiri (2008) provide a few examples; Lanzenberger, Sampson, and Rester (2009), Abbasi and Chen (2007), Le Bœuf, Martinez, and Aitken (2005), and Castro, Rocha da Silva, and Ribeiro (2014), among many others, combine the *content* of the texts as well as *metadata* from the data structures containing the text for richer visualizations.

The partnership of data + design still tends to reflect the creators' arts or science background. Their offspring results in fascinating visualizations. In the *Lord of the Rings Project*, Tolkien's works have been parsed and the data shared among several projects (common words, sentiment analysis, character co-occurrence), along with other graphics to support the appropriate affective quality of the works (see http://lotrproject.com/statistics/books/).

Information visualization in this book has focused on the role of communication between the image and the viewer. InfoVis is also used to study sense making and encourage public engagement. Heer, Viégas, & Wattenberg (2007) applied visualizations to "report the results of user studies of the system, observing emergent patterns of social data analysis, including cycles of observation and hypothesis, and the complementary roles of social navigation and data-driven exploration" (p. 1029). An institution offering interactive visualizations that are open to public engagement and discussion creates a digital agora, a sphere of stimulation for discussion, as well as provides data for its own discourse analysis of the attitudes, linguistic register, and trends among user groups.

Information visualizations do not have to be boring! Creative visual interpretations, in light of the guidelines above, yield a wonderful marriage of data, art, and the user. Stefanie Posavec (http://www.stefanieposavec.com/design/) and many others invite you to check them out. The volume and variety of these data speak strongly for the interactive, exploratory nature of contemporary visualization to *help us turn data into meaningful information.*

REFERENCES

Abbasi, A., & Chen, H. (2007). Categorization and analysis of text in computer mediated communication archives using visualization. *JCDL '07 Proceedings of the 7th ACM/IEEE-CS Joint Conference on Digital Libraries*, 11–18.

Benoît, G., & Agarwal, N. (2012). All-visual retrieval: How people search and respond to an affect-driven visual information retrieval system. *Proceedings of the American Society of Information Science and Technology, 49*(1), 1–4.

Benoît, G., & Hussey, L. (2011). Repurposing digital objects: Case studies across the publishing industry. *JASIST, 62*(2), 363–374.

Brath, R., & Banissi, E. (2014). Using font attributes in knowledge maps and information retrieval. *Proceedings of the First Workshop on Knowledge Maps and Information*

Retrieval (KMIR 2014), co-located with International Conference on Digital Libraries (DL 2014), 23–30.

Castro, J., Rocha da Silva, J., & Ribeiro, C. (2014). Creating lightweight ontologies for dataset description: Practice applications in a cross-domain research data management workflow. *IEEE/ACM Joint Conference on Digital Libraries*, 313–316.

Ghorbel, F., Ellouze, N., Metais, E., Hamdi, F., Gargouri, F., & Herradi, N. (2016.). Memo graph: An ontology visualization tool for everyone. *Procedia Computer Science, 96*, 265–274.

Hartnett, K. (2015, April 8). Teaching scientists how to visualize their data. *Boston Globe*. Retrieved from https://www.bostonglobe.com/ideas/2015/04/08/teaching-scientists -how-visualize-their-data/XI6b7xZPRGD3veJcLPl10H/story.html

Heer, J., Viégas, F. B., & Watenberg, M. (2007). Voyagers and voyeurs: Supporting asyn- chronous collaborative information visualization. *CHI 2007 Proceedings—Distributed Interaction*, pp. 1029–38.

Huisman, R., Miller, M., & Trinoskey, J. (2011). We've Wordled, have you?: Digital images in the library classroom. *C&RL News, 72*(9). Retrieved from https://crln.acrl.org /index.php/crlnews/article/view/8634/9056#b3-0720522

Kucher, K., & Kerren, A. (2015). Text visualization techniques: Taxonomy, visual survey, and community insights. *Visualization symposium (PacificVis) 2015*. Hangzhou, China. Retrieved from https://ieeexplore.ieee.org/document/7156366/

Lanzenberger, M., Sampson, J., & Rester, M. (2009). Visualization in ontology tools. *2009 International Conference on Complex, Intelligent and Software Intensive Systems*, IEEE.

Le Bœuf, P., Martinez, K., & Aitken, G. (2005). Using an ontology for interoperability and browsing of museum, library and archive information. *ICOM Committee for Conser- vation, 1*, 1–6.

Lindquist, T., & Gilman, T. (2008, January). Academic research librarians with subject doc- torates: Data and trends, 1965–2006. *University Libraries Faculty and Staff Contribu- tions, 3*. Retrieved from https://scholar.colorado.edu/libr_facpapers/3

Link, V., Lohmann, E. M., Negru, S., & Wiens, V. (2018). WebVowl. Retrieved from http:// vowl.visualdataweb.org/webvowl.html

Rios, J. (2017). Visualization tools. Harvard Law School Library. Retrieved May 29, 2018, from https://guides.library.harvard.edu/c.php?g=310952&p=2073191

Shiri, A. (2008). Metadata-enhanced visual interfaces to digital libraries. *Journal of Infor- mation Science, 34*(6), 763–775.

Stockinger, P. (2015). The semiotic turn in digital archives and libraries. *Les Cahiers du Numerique, 1*, 4.

Viégas, F. B., Wattenberg, M., & Feinberg, J. (2009). Participatory visualization with Wordle. *IEEE Transactions on Visualization and Computer Graphics, 15*(6), 1137–1144.

Data and Information Ecosystems

The world of InfoVis seems to divide into two friendly camps: those favoring back-end data, including cleaning and analysis, with a visualization as a layer on top of the data; and those favoring user experience (aesthetics, graphics, interactivity) over the already prepared data stores. But as popular tools such as Apple's Numbers spreadsheet software, which integrates interactive donut visualizations and statistical software, add more visualization power, the next logical step is to teach data-oriented people more about graphics and interactivity and teach graphics-focused people more about data analysis.

This appendix reviews main points about data preparation and analysis. Naturally, we cannot completely review the breadth and depth of this vital activity.

CONTENTS

A VIEW OF DATA

We can categorize data into three types: structured, semistructured, and unstructured. *Structured data* are those stored in a relational database. These include data in cells; the cells are named facets such as "last_name" and arranged in a row to create a single record.

Semistructured data are stored in "flat files," text files that can be read by any computer. The semistructuring is based on how those text data are arranged in the file. Some examples are SwissProt records, which are used in biomedical research. While the content is all text, the text is arranged according to strict rules and section titles. It is fairly easy to extract data from these files. A more common example includes .xml and .json files. The addition of semantic tags in .xml and use of brackets in .json facilitate identifying the parent-child relationships in the data and extracting the data needed.

Unstructured data is everything else. Full-text search engines, text mining, and contemporary "information ecologies" such as Hadoop and MapReduce parse full-text files. The data to be visualized usually consist of very large sets of data drawn from multiple resources and so ought to be prepared into (a) a homogeneous data type and (b) "cleaned" of data that may cause unnecessary errors. The data store should not have null values, values that are patently out of the usual domain of the data.

DATA CLEANING AND MINING

If our information needs were satisfied only by the discovery of known entities through querying of structured databases, then there would be no need to mine the data. The purpose of data mining (DM) is to explore databases for the unknown, by exposing patterns from the data that are novel, or "determining their interestingness," supporting these patterns through statistical evidence, and presenting these results to the user via a graphic interface that facilitates investigation and interpretation to guide or support actions. DM relies on sophisticated mathematical and statistical models, and substantial computing power, to help users convert algorithmic behavior to human-understandable rules for action. For example, say a pharmaceutical company develops a new drug that it wants to market. With no information about to whom to market the drug, the company turns to sales records as evidence of past purchasing behavior, to discover which clients might be interested in the new product. Such data may be stored in a relational database, but standard SQL queries are unproductive. The firm may query the database for "which distributors in the Boston area purchased beta blockers?" but not "which distributors in the Boston area are likely to purchase this new drug and why?" DM assists in the automated discovery of patterns and may establish association rules to be interpreted by the end user: "If a company distributes beta blocker X and has sales of over \$$Y$ per year in the Boston area, the likelihood of that company purchasing the new drug is Z percent."

This same firm may have a research arm that generates technical reports, clinical trial data, and other nonstructured records. Searching these types of flat files and weakly typed sources is not possible with SQL queries, and full-text retrieval methods may not be useful because the researchers do not have a query (or hypotheses) to answer. Here DM techniques are applied to discover patterns and suggest to the researchers a basis for further investigation. See Benoît (2005) for a complete description with illustrations.

Brachman and Anand (1996) note that there is no systematized DM methodology, although major steps can be identified:

- Getting to know the data and the task: this stage is more significant than it sounds, especially when the data is to be pulled from multiple sources and when the analysis will not be done by the business user.
- Acquisition: bringing the data into the appropriate environment for analysis.
- Integration and checking: confirming the expected form and broad content of the data, and integrating the data into tools as required.
- Data cleaning: looking for obvious flaws in the data and removing them, and removing records with errors or insignificant outliers.
- Model and hypothesis development: simple exploration of the data through passive techniques and elaboration by deriving new data attributes where necessary; selection of an appropriate model to perform analysis; and development of initial hypotheses to test.
- Data mining: application of the core discovery procedures to reveal patterns and new knowledge or to verify hypotheses developed prior to this step.
- Testing and verification: assessing the discovered knowledge, including testing predictive models on test sets and analyzing segmentation.
- Interpretation and use: integration with existing domain knowledge, which may confirm, deny, or challenge the newly discovered patterns.

Typically a subject specialist, working with a data analyst, refines the problem to be resolved. In what is termed *verification-driven*, or *top-down*, *data mining*, the problem to be resolved is pursued by posing a standard query (e.g., "what are the sales in Chicago for 2001?"). The result of these SQL queries generates a kind of cross-tabulation report based on the predetermined structure of the database. The next step is to run appropriate machine-learning (ML) algorithms, or combinations of algorithms. This step may entail repeatedly altering the selection and representation of data. For instance, the miner may segment the data based on a hypothesis that a set of properties (e.g., median age, income, and ZIP code) form an appropriate group for a direct mail campaign, but may alter the selection of properties if nothing interpretable is generated.

Alternatively, the miner may not have a hypothesis and so asks the system to create one (called *predictive*, *discovery-driven*, or *bottom-up data mining*, e.g., "do sales for beta blockers in the Chicago area outpace those in the Los Angeles area?"). The DM system either proves or disproves it through statistical regression.

But to achieve this end, the data must have been previously selected and cleaned, determining the granularity of each data type. For instance, does the "Chicago area" include the geographic limits of that city, or all markets served from Chicago area ZIP codes? Will a distributor's sales be represented by a category (e.g., $1–2 million sales per annum) or a value (e.g., $1,400,000)?

In both situations, a DM application may first classify or cluster the data through some artificial intelligence (AI) algorithms (of which artificial neural networks are most common), into a self-organizing map from which cause-and-effect association rules can be established. For instance, by clustering histories of credit card purchases of high-fashion clothing from a six-month period, it is possible to determine which customers are likely to purchase related luxury products. By altering the underlying statistical model, it is also possible to have neural networks build nonlinear predictive models. For example, it can be determined which graduate school marketing campaign is likely to draw which types of applicants, regardless of the candidates' past academic performance.

The generated association rules also include probabilities. In Date's example (2000, p. 722) of a customer buying shoes, the association rule suggests that socks will be purchased, too; for all transactions

tx (shoes $\in tx \wedge$ all socks $\in tx$) where "shoes $\in tx$" is the rule antecedent and "socks $\in tx$" is the rule consequent, and tx ranges overall sales transactions,

the probability of both purchases occurring in the same sale is x percent.

Association rules provide the user with two additional statistics: support and confidence. Support is the fraction of the population that satisfies the rule; confidence is that set of the population in which the antecedent and the consequent is satisfied. In Date's socks and shoes example, the population is 4, the support is 50 percent, and the confidence is 66.6 percent. The end user is fairly confident in interpreting the association as "if a customer buys shoes, he is likely to buy socks as well, though not necessarily in the same transaction." The decision-making knowledge (or heuristic) of the domain specialist helps in avoiding derived correlations that, for a specific data mining activity, may be useless. These include the "known but trivial" (people who buy shoes will buy socks), "chance" (the shoes and a shirt were on the same sale), and "unknown but trivial" (brown shoes were purchased with black ones).

Association rules may be time-dependent or sequential. For example, the purchases of a customer base may be grouped into sales periods (e.g., spring sale, summer white sale, pre-school fall sale), and sequential algorithms may determine that if children's beachwear is purchased in the spring sale, there's an 80 percent chance that school clothing will be purchased during the fall sale.

Besides association and sequencing, other main processes include classification and clustering, which are performed by specific computing algorithms. These techniques are grouped based on how they treat the data: by correlating or finding relationships between the records (e.g., neural networks, link-analysis), by partitioning the data (e.g., decision trees and rules, example-based nearest-neighbor classification, case-based reasoning, decision trellises), by recording deviations (deviation detection, nonlinear regression), and other techniques (inductive logic and hybrid multi-strategy techniques, such as combining rule induction and case-based reasoning).

Finally, to profit from data mining activities, the human analyst, a domain expert, must be able to interpret the results of the model in a manner appropriate for that field: trends have emerged where certain industries have settled on customary ways of presenting data. The data mining output consequently must fit into this framework. Significantly, this includes aesthetic and graphic-design decisions being made for *us*. This is not entirely a bad thing, although our perspective is that the designer of the visualization must "own" all facets of the visualization—data, graphics, aesthetics, and interactivity. The results of the calculations are visualized on-screen, displaying complex multidimensional data, often in three-dimensional renderings. Such visualization software is intended to give the user a mental framework for interpreting the data.

The basic DM processes described above incorporate several assumptions about the size and quality of the data, the knowledge of the end user, and the computing environment. However, these assumptions cannot be taken for granted as DM evolves.

Data

All data mining activities are founded on the properties and representations of the data. As DM tools have no built-in semantic model of the data, users must take necessary precautions to ensure that the data are "cleaned," or in a state that minimizes errors based on the data. Addressing the issue of missing values and inconsistent, noisy, and redundant data is part of the data cleaning process. In situations where nuisance data cannot be eliminated or probabilistically determined, DM requires more sophisticated statistical strategies to compensate by identifying variables and dependencies. However, data that are mined using compensating mathematical methods risk overfitting the data to the model, that is, accidentally selecting the best parameters for one particular model. Thus, preparing data for mining entails a certain amount of risk and therefore must be carefully performed.

Miners must determine record usability (Wright, 1996) and preprocess data to a fixed form, such as binary or ordered variables. However, there are times when data may not be mapped to a standard form, such as when processing free text where replicated fields may be missed. Similarly, many DM methods are designed around ordered numerical values and cannot easily process categorical data. Users who attempt to standardize their data through any number of methods (normalization, decimal scaling, standard deviation normalization, and data smoothing) may be able to improve feature selection but may accidentally introduce new errors. For instance, when measures are small, neural networks often train well, but if not normalized, distance measures for nearest-neighbor calculations overweight those features. Moreover, the miner must ensure that the normalization applied to the training set is also applied to mined data. Some methods, such as neural networks and regression trees, have smoothers implicit in their representation and perform well for prediction. Smoothing also may reduce the search space by discretizing continuous features into a set of discrete features, covering a fixed range of values.

Here we discuss some responses to data mining of continuous, missing, and reduced datasets. Continuous variables are often discretized, although it may entail a loss of information value. In the pharmaceutical company example, the marketing group may convert the volume of sales into discrete groups of "high" and "low" volume. This may help the sales force conceptualize the question, although it may degrade the DM process. In neural networks, for instance, input parameters that are not scaled or coded appropriately impact learning ability. The simplest method is to divide the range into units of equal width. Miners must be aware of the risk of losing information about the relationship between preassigned classes and interval boundaries when discretizing.

One solution for missing data is to predict the values from other data. Such surrogate techniques are possible, such as when using decision trees, but the answer is not simple. Some missing values may be null, but they may not be applicable to the task. This situation arises where heterogeneous databases are mined because the relational model requires all types in a relation to have the same number of attributes. For example, in selecting a patient group for possible inclusion in a clinical trial, some missing data attributes may be estimated based on other examples for which the value is known. In growing a decision tree, the miner assigns a common value to a missing attribute, calculated from the entire set or projected from other members within a cluster. The missing data may also be assigned a probability of all possible values and then re-estimated based on observed frequencies of other values within the training set.

Similar to the case of continuous values, missing data in neural networks are difficult to detect and prevent the network from converging. This is a situation where both domain expert and analyst should work together and where most DM applications fail to provide more interactive opportunities for users.

Another avenue for resolving missing data, or addressing uncertainty, by prediction comes from fuzzy sets and rough sets. Rough sets expose hidden deterministic rules in databases and can be expanded to extract probabilistic rules. The generalized rough-set model can be applied where data are missing, or when users provide a range for the data, which addresses a great challenge for DM. There is an interaction between rough sets, data mining, granular-soft computing, and fuzzy sets for time-dependent linguistic systems, something that might first suggest using hidden Markov models.

Another data-centered technique to improve computer efficiency minimizes the size of the dataset before processing. Data reduction is performed to reduce the size of the search space, or to remove fields that do not contribute to increasing the efficiency of the mining algorithm or which contribute in insignificant ways. Reducing the data requires careful, validated selection of properties which are redundant, and so do not contribute to increasing effectiveness or information gain, and do not accidentally make the new data to be mined unrecognizable when compared to the training set.

One method is *feature selection*, a pre-pruning, inductive learning process. Feature selection both improves computation speed and the quality of classification. Users may want to select the "best" features of their data when there are a large number of features, or when calculating standard errors is computationally intensive. Simplification improves computer time, but users may tend to select the features to best suit their model instead of working more with the data. For example, in decision-tree learning, methods are developed that stop growing the tree earlier—before it reaches the point where it classifies perfectly the dataset, and instead allows the tree to overfit the data and then prune the resulting rule set. The latter case may be preferable because the rule set is more interpretable to the end user.

Additionally, smaller sets increase the system's ability to test hypotheses. If the smaller set yields good results, it may be possible to bypass other tests on the entire dataset. Inexperienced miners may mistake good-looking sets for valid results, and skip confirmatory tests (Elder, 2000). A reduction method based on smaller sets, on the other hand, can and should be subjected to confirmatory algorithms because the set can be efficiently manipulated. This also suggests that small sets may be appropriate for distributed systems, which later can take the aggregate for a final output.

Data reduction techniques vary depending on the learning algorithm. For example, when reducing data for neural networks, the inputs must be fitted to a range, usually 0 to 1. The transformation choice will impact the training of the system. Inappropriate reduction introduces outliers, which in turn skews distributions and causes the network to perform poorly.

Algorithms

Algorithm design stressing computational efficiency has become a critical issue for data mining, for several reasons. One is that most "first-generation algorithms" assume certain properties of the data, such as fitting into a single computer's memory or dealing only with numeric and symbolic data. Another reason is the difficulty of learning rules from extremely large databases. DM algorithms also assume that the data have been carefully prepared before being subjected to largely automated rule production systems, minimizing the human end user's interactive role. For example, algorithms designed for small search spaces may generate spurious associations when applied to large, distributed, or parallel sources, which might be handled more effectively if the user's knowledge were incorporated at key stages. The task in algorithm design, then, is how to accommodate diverse sources of data, increases in the number of records and attributes per observation, derived rule sets used to analyze the collection, and how to increase user participation. Some of the developments are outlined below.

Agent-based approaches are software applications programmed to investigate and collect data on their own. These intelligent agents prowl the Internet, relying on user profiles and user-supplied information about the subject (e.g., medical data) and document types of interest. PADMA, Harvest, ParaSite, OCCAM, and FAQ Finder systems are examples. More interactive agents, such as the Internet shopping tool ShopBot, interact with and learn from unfamiliar information sources.

Association or *rule induction* procedures come originally from the retail industry, such as analyzing customers' account portfolios, to express item affinities in terms of confidence-rated rules, and have been adapted to many situations. Indeed, a most active area in DM research is improving the efficiency and removing redundancy of association and classification rules. Association rule production is not efficient with continuous classes, or when there are many intervals in the data. In response, fuzzy techniques improve predictions, but degrade the end user's ability to comprehend the generated rules.

Clustering, often the first step in DM, assigns database records with many shared attributes into smaller segments, or clusters. DM systems automatically identify distinguishing characteristics and assign records to an *n*-dimensional space. This is common in demographic-based market analysis. In image databases, clustering can be used to detect interesting spatial patterns and support content-based retrievals of images and videos using low-level features such as texture, color histogram, shape descriptions, etc. (Manjunath, 2001) Good clustering techniques maximize the cluster membership while minimizing accidental membership, by applying either supervised or unsupervised AI techniques. The algorithms used in clustering must examine all data points, determine potential clustering features, and refine cluster membership, or classifier generation and classifier application. As the size of the database grows, the likelihood of outliers also grows, requiring some means of removing irrelevant dimensions, such as feature selection or pruning. A popular technique is *k*-means, which randomly picks *k* data points as cluster centers and assigns new points to clusters in terms of squared error or Euclidean distance. The challenge is scaling *k*-means clustering. Through multiple additive regression, scaled *k*-means clustering offers secondary validation and may be applied to parallel and distributed DM environments. For large datasets, there are methods of creating "candidate *k*-itemsets," a minimized frequent itemset such as those used in market-based analysis.

Classification of data is arguably the most important function and the most commonly applied technique. Classification employs a set of predetermined examples to develop a model to categorize population of records to predefine the similarity of neighbors before machine-learning techniques are employed. A typical use is fraud detection and credit-risk applications. Classification employs some form of supervised learning method such as decision trees, neural networks, DNF rules, Bayesian classifiers, and genetic algorithms to predict the membership of new records.

Another typical technique is nearest-neighbor classifiers, which use a training set to measure the similarity (or distance function) of all -tuples and then attempts an analysis on the test data. Variations include *k* nearest neighbors (which classifies each record based on a combination of classes of *k* records that are most similar to it in the dataset), weighted voting of nearest neighbors, and edited nearest neighbor. Mining of heterogeneous sources requires updated distance-measurement functions.

Decision trees are a popular top-down approach to classification that divides the dataset into leaf and node divisions (a "recursive partitioning approach") until the entire set has been analyzed. Growing the tree usually employs CART (classification and regression) and CHAID (chi-squared automatic interaction detection). Each interval node in the tree represents a decision on an attribute, which splits the database into two or more children. Decision trees are popular because they process both qualitative and quantitative data in an efficient and accurate manner. For qualitative attributes, the set of outcomes is the set of different values in the respective attribute domain; quantitative attributes rely on a specific threshold value that is assigned by the user to generate different branches. This greedy search over the entire search space for all possible trees is computationally very intense and, in light of the huge size of databases, becoming nearly impossible to perform. There are other related techniques that seek the "best" test attribute, such as nearest-neighbor classifiers that handle only a few hundred -tuples, entropy, and information gain, which are mentioned in passing for the sake of completeness but cannot be addressed further here.

Note that other techniques are useful. Each of the following have mature literature, too vast to include in this review, although these techniques are important in DM. Very popular in business and classification, *artificial neural networks* are nonlinear predictive models that learn from a prepared dataset and then are applied to new, larger sets. *Genetic algorithms* (GAs), like neural networks, are based on biological functions. GAs work by incorporating mutation and natural selection and have been applied in scalable data mining. An offspring of genetic-based mining, *genetic programming*, is also employed (Wong, 2000). *Sequence-based analysis* is time-dependent, such as when the purchase of one item might predict subsequent purchases. *Graphic models* and *hierarchical probabilistic representations* are directed graph models, generalized Markov models, and hidden Markov models. These techniques are usually employed in conjunction with others, among them case-based reasoning, fuzzy logic, fractal-based transforms, lattice, and rough sets.

Software Applications Implement the Algorithms

The computing platform that stores, manipulates, examines, and presents the data must be sufficiently powerful or be provided with efficiently designed software. This is an important issue in DM because it often involves considerable computing overhead to perform iterative data analyses and complex, interactive visualization.

The software used in data mining may be categorized based on the application's operation: generic, single-task; generic, multitask; and application-specific. Generic, single-task applications emphasize classification (decision trees, neural networks, example-based, rule-discovery). These applications require significant pre- and postprocessing by the user, typically a developer who integrates these approaches as part of a complete application. Generic, multitask systems support a variety of discovery tasks, typically combining several classification techniques, query and retrieval, clustering, and visualization. Multitask DM systems are designed primarily for users who understand data manipulation.

Application-specific tools, on the other hand, are employed by domain specialists, people trained in a field, say bioinformatics, but who know little about the process of analysis. Such miners therefore rely more heavily on the software to validate patterns detected in the data and to guide in the interpretation of results.

HADOOP, SPARK, AND MAPREDUCE

Data mining activities are part of the back-end of information visualization, and information visualization is part of the broader understanding of data and text mining. The tighter integration of computer network architectures to support very large stores of files (hence "big data"), cleaning, and working with data to create visualizations for understanding have led to a number of important trends.

One is the Apache Hadoop (http://hadoop.apache.org/) project. The Apache Hadoop project develops free open source software for reliable, scalable, distributed computing.

The Apache Hadoop software library is a framework that allows for the distributed processing of large datasets across clusters of computers using simple programming models. It is designed to scale up from single servers to thousands of machines, each offering local computation and storage. Rather than rely on hardware to deliver high availability, the library itself is designed to detect and handle failures at the application layer, therefore delivering a highly available service on top of a cluster of computers, each of which may be prone to failures.

Hadoop includes a number of subprojects, such as HDFS (Hadoop Distributed File System) and MapReduce, a system for parallel processing of large datasets. MapReduce is very similar to full-text and text mining activities, and leads to counts of semantic tokens. The clustering and counting of raw text data reduces the volume of data to be passed to the next level of processing. An alternative to MapReduce is Spark. Spark is considerably faster in processing data files and supports some machine-learning and graphing utilities. For more, check out Kardi Teknomo's MapReduce tutorial at https://people.revoledu.com/kardi/tutorial/DataScience/MapReduce.html.

SUMMARY

Data must be prepared—cleaned, analyzed, made computationally more efficient—before visualization can occur. There are noticeable improvements in computational speed when data are sorted and clustered before further processing.

REFERENCES

Benoît, G. (2005). Data mining. In B. Cronin (Ed.), *Annual Review of Information Science and Technology* (ARIST), vol. 36 (pp. 265–310). Medford, NJ: Wiley.

Brachman, R. J. & Anand, T. (1996). The process of knowledge discovery in databases. *Advances in knowledge discovery and data mining.* Menlo Park: Amer. Association for Artificial Intelligence, p. 37–57.

Date, C. J. (2000). *An introduction to database systems.* New York: Addison-Wesley.

Elder, J. F. (2000). *Top 10 data mining mistakes.* Available from http://www.datamininglab.com

Manjunath, B. S., et al. (2001, June). Color and texture descriptors. *IEEE transactions on circuits and systems for video technology*, Vol. 11(6), 703–15.

Wong, S. V., & Hamouda, A. M. S. (2000, April). Optimization of fuzzy rules design using genetic algorithm. *Journal of advanced engineering software 31*(4), 251–62.

Wright, M. (1996). The dubious assumptions of segmentation and targeting. *Management decision, 34*(1), 18–24.

More about Data, Learning, and Visualization

A cardinal function of information visualization is to support exposing unanticipated relationships in the data. We have reviewed some aspects of data preparation before visualization, and we now need to address how the data themselves contribute to being discovered. Machine learning (ML) and artificial intelligence (AI) have been active research and practice areas for many decades, but it is only in the 2010s that AI has pervaded the popular press about technology and society. In this appendix we review in more detail some of the ML and AI activities and how they map to the front end of visualizations. Clearly we cannot approach the depth nor the breadth of machine learning, but we can introduce some concepts that help associate data and their presentation. Check out https://stackoverflow.com /questions/32739772/d3-vs-scipy-voronoi-diagram-implementation for a comparison of d3 and scipy Voronoi diagrams.

DATA'S RELATIONSHIP TO INFOVIS

In all scenarios of big data and learning, there is a graphic component. Here we see where data visualization and information visualization converge and diverge. On the one hand, there exists a tremendous number of mathematical and statistical software applications that facilitate data cleaning and graphing. Once graphed, the resulting visualization might not be shareable (for example, the graph cannot be exported except as a static image), the end user might not have an opportunity to interact with the visualization to learn more after the initial purpose of the data analysis, and the aesthetics might not cohere with the message to be found in the data, nor with the intended audience. The complexity of these applications restrict their use to the specialist. The emphasis is on the data, the mathematical models that extract potentially useful data subsets (aka "moments" or "interesting events"). Commercial tools perform a lot of the heavy lifting of the data and remove many of the programmers' responsibilities when creating an information visualization; d3.js controls all aspects of the user experience, but does not address data cleaning and algorithms. d3 and others require the dataset to be cleaned and prepared.

On the other hand, machine learning is modeled on how people supposedly learn from life. The examples of automatic topic extraction, clustering, classification, and decision trees generally mimic how people learn through "concept learning." Despite today's detractors, concept learning gained popularity in the early twentieth century and continues to influence researchers. For example, people may be taught to identify something, as a parent might instruct a child, and then shore up the identification with life experiences. By extension, people apply some facet from the earlier learning to understanding something novel. In 1920, Hull (see University of Indiana, 2017), applied this stimulus-response to learning Chinese ideographs. Bruner, Goodnow, and Austin (2009) detail the idea of "necessary" features for people to identify a concept; for example, to be a canary necessitates the concept and expression of "yellow." In arts education, language learning, and computing, such rule-based categories are popular. In concept learning, given a set of rules, people cluster items based on several conjunctive, disjunctive, conditional, and biconditional categories.

"We may speak of a 'category' of instances or a concept in terms of the defining properties of some subset of the instances. For example, 'all cards with one red figure' is a concept, so too 'all cards with two figures and/or with circles,' so too 'all cards possessing the same number of figures and borders.' . . . A *conjunctive category* is one defined by the *joint presence* of the appropriate value of several attributes" (Bruner et al., 2009, p. 41). Imagine a deck of cards with only red hearts showing. We might define this as the conjunction of three figures: redness, shapes (king, heart, etc.), and suit. Bruner and colleagues (2009, p. 41) continue, "The *disjunctive category* may be illustrated by that class of cards that possess three red circles, or any constituent therefore: three figures, red figures, circles, three red figures, red circles, or three circles." By taking the "whole" of the category and identifying subclasses, using a deck of cards we can create 57 instances of a disjunctive category. The reduction of the theories of thinking for our purposes is to emphasize that how people *think* about associations is based on a variety of properties. As visualization designers, we may not anticipate how viewers parse the visualization—that is, what they will identify for their thinking, such as color and shape versus size and placement. As a viewer reflects on the identified categories, he or she will project conditions under which the set member could be true ("conditional"); and there can be equally biconditional, where some factor dominates to justify the interpretation. In figure Appendix B.1, we start with + and − to show membership in a given category. Given the set of three shapes and three colors, how tight is the rearrangement based on our thinking (Chater, Lyon, & Myers, 1990)?

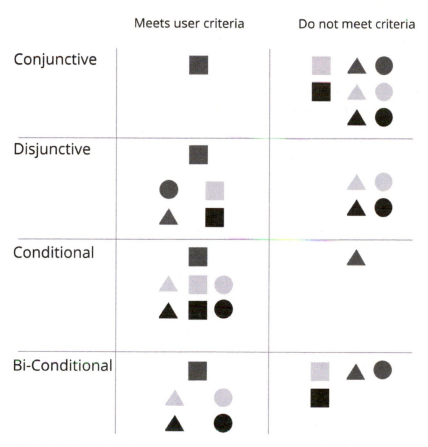

FIGURE APPENDIX B.1 Ways in which users might conceptually cluster data representations of different shapes and colors. *Courtesy of the author*

But when we turn to more realistic graphic shapes, such as icons, faces, or other realistic symbols, people may learn by family resemblance or prototypes. Of course, there are situational factors, as well as mutable cultural ones, that affect categorization and resemblances. When should we apply prototyping? Should a set of circles, for instance, be grouped more by their size or their color? Depending on the specific circumstance, we can gain or can lose potential informing qualities about objects by how the shapes are arranged or by how they tell different stories. Posner and Keele compare techniques and conclude that people categorize new items when they do not know the rules by putting a new item in the category with the most similar exemplars. Yet the principle underlying the difference between data visualization and information visualization is the role of the viewer's cognition, transforming data by projecting scenarios that the viewer can comprehend and for which she or he can see an application.

Hierarchical Organization of Concepts

One technique for organizing concepts is to establish a basic level of symbols and message. This is akin to the ISO12696 linguistic register's baseline. From the basic level, which is the level most immediately recognizable by viewers, people can identify subsets (or subordinate) symbols or words below the level of basic. Likewise, they recognize the larger class of objects to which the basic level can belong. This creates a hierarchy that aids in creating and mapping the design toward how people interpret the relationships among symbols.

How do people know which objects or terms are the basic level and which are related terms that are subordinate (more specific) or superordinate? People tend toward the basic level of an object, the shortest name, and will be more comfortable with the basic object as new features are introduced. When designing a visualization or graphic and applying the three levels of superordinate, basic, and subordinate, the viewer will have more difficulty disambiguating the contents of the visual message if the design emphasizes the superordinate level. There would not be enough recognizable elements for the viewer to begin to construct a "mental model," because too many subelements might apply. Designing an InfoVis starting at the basic level facilitates establishing a baseline for interpretation. Starting at the subordinate level with lots of very specific common elements, the viewer may rather quickly identify a common theme associating all the elements. For example, if designing a visualization about animals, the three levels might be "mammals" as the superordinate level, "pets" as the basic level, and specific "dogs and cats" at the subordinate level. There are too many potential interpretations and not enough detail for the viewer to comprehend the data should the design emphasize "mammals." On the other hand, starting with "pets" or "dogs and cats," the interpretive options are restricted. This means we can "present and explain" the data; by adding interactive tools so that the viewer can change the dimensionality of the data, moving from one level to another, we step closer to the "exploratory" feature of an InfoVis. If we start at too subordinate a level, people recognize the object and can progress back to the basic level (Rosch, Mervis, Gray, Johnson, & Boyes-Braem, 1976). Tennyson and Cocchiarella (1986) and Klausmeier (1980) systematized concepts by establishing a concrete idea in the viewer's mind, revising the relationship between the unknown and the existing knowledge by recalling examples or improving the reasons for the association between them, and classifying the potential new knowledge, either by noting a classification rule (Tennyson & Cocchiarella, 1986) or classifying with a further step of formalizing the knowledge by applying it to new circumstances (Klausmeier, 1980).

Finally, we return to an elementary model of what we might add and what we might extract from the data when preparing it through cleaning, mapping, and processing. Each of these processes from perception to data and back again should be familiar to information professionals, as seen in figure Appendix B.2.

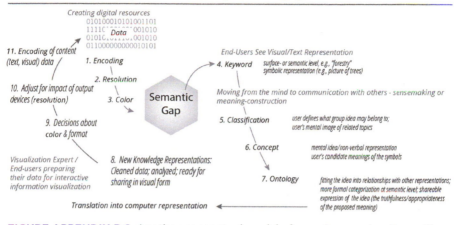

SENSEMAKING LIFECYCLE:
integrating usual semantic gap with (a) visual languages, (b) end-user progress - from initial exposure to semantics (text or visual), (c) to creating digital resource for sharing in a visual language.

FIGURE APPENDIX B.2 Another conceptual model of meaning construction with visual data from a data-to-user life cycle. *Courtesy of the author*

Let's consider visual examples. The horizontal bubble chart in figure Appendix B.3 could be cast as a basic-level concept because of all the industries on the stock market (superordinate level), the chart is restricted to S&P 500 ("basic" level). The composite bubble chart (figure Appendix B.4) has "sector views" that can be cast as the subordinate level.

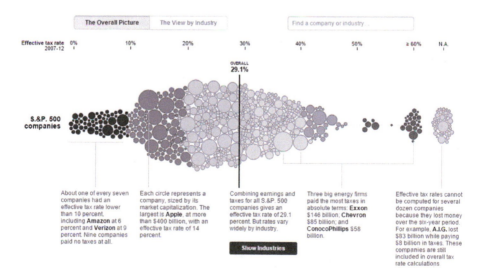

FIGURE APPENDIX B.3 An interactive visualization combining simultaneously superordinate and subordinate levels of data. *Courtesy of the author*

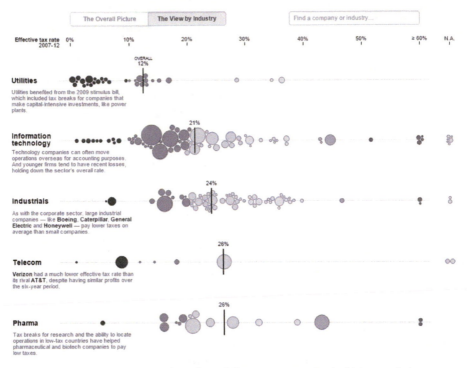

FIGURE APPENDIX B.4 Another view of the same complex bubble graph, here demonstrating subordinate level data. *Courtesy of the author*

CODE LIBRARIES AND VISUALIZATION

Most programming languages have an option to view the values of variables, data types, results of calculations, and so on, without having to compile a program or interpret a script. For example, JavaScript will echo to a browser's console window (in the "Show source" option). IDEs (integrated development environments) for Java and other languages also allow peeking at the code to help debugging (e.g., NetBeans, JBuilder, Eclipse, XCode, PyCharm). Python implementations include interactive interfaces, helper tools like Jupyter Notebook, and the larger multi-application support tool, Anaconda. Jupyter facilitates writing code and sharing it with others in the form of an interactive "notebook."

The Python programmer benefits enormously by importing libraries that address data preparation, mathematical calculations, visualization tools in general, and task-specific tools. One useful tool is pprint ("pretty printer"), a library to ease the formatting of Python output (https://docs.python.org/3/library/pprint.html). Another is xlrd, a library for extracting data from Microsoft Excel spreadsheets (https://pypi.python.org/pypi/xlrd).

Here are some utilities common in data science work:

- d3.js: very popular JavaScript library for interactive data documents/visualizations; visit https://d3js.org and check out the gallery
- IPython (interactive Python): https://ipython.org
- Jupyter (Python shareable notebooks): jupyter.org
- Anaconda: https://anaconda.org/anaconda/python
- NumPy: www.numpy.org
- matplotlib (python 2d plotting library)https://matplotlib.org
- R with ggplot and ggvis: https://www.r-project.org/, http://ggplot2.org, https://ggvis.rstudio.com
- scrapy—for scrapping web content ("spiders"): https://scrapy.org
- Beautiful Soup: https://www.crummy.com/software/BeautifulSoup/
- Seaborn (graphing): https://seaborn.pydata.org—graphing
- Pandas (data analysis toolkit, easy handling of missing values, especially for series data and DataFrames): https://pandas.pydata.org/pandas-docs /stable/
- altair (declarative visualization charts): https://altair-viz.github.io
- holoviews (chart-making kit): http://holoviews.org
- scikit learn (an astonishing product for machine learning, including OCR and face recognition tools): http://scikit-learn.org/stable/
- Bokeh: http://bokeh.pydata.org/en/latest/
- Java (a programming language with many graphing and effects libraries): https://www.java.com/en/

A couple of tools serve as examples of the larger visual information ecology. Python is not the only powerful tool in your arsenal. Java is a full-featured programming language with many built-in libraries facilitating data preparation. Visit https://www.java.com/en/ to learn more. There is also an interactive visualization environment for Java called "Jive" (https://www.cse.buffalo.edu/jive/).

Each of these tools contributes to your advancement in programming. As often noted, learning programming from a book or an online tutorial introduces only the basics. To advance your knowledge of the topic, the best way is to set yourself a programming task. Breaking down and detailing the logical steps (called process decomposition) results in a suite of related "pseudocode" or "structured English" modules. As you write the pseudocode, you'll encounter more details about what the program or script requires (improving your analysis skills), and working with your manual or tutorial will teach you which functions or objects to use or how to write your own. From there, it is possible to gain a clearer view of the relationship of the programming to the end user experience, the relationship potential in the data, and how to map the whole to the interactive InfoVis.

Figure Appendix B.5 is a familiar model of the client-server architecture seen from a machine-learning programmers' perspective. Broadly stated, step 1 is a data-gathering activity, here using "scraping" websites for their content and then storing the data, probably as a .json file, on a server or database. The second step cleans the data—null values, data clearly out of range, perhaps reduce dimensionality, add labels or metadata to the data points—to ensure a warehouse of data suitable for further investigation. Step 3 focuses on the data analysis and extraction of data to help discover new trends or facts in the data. Steps 4 and 5 deliver the data to the end users' browsers for interactive visualization. What are some of the specifics of data, machine learning, visualization, and the end user?

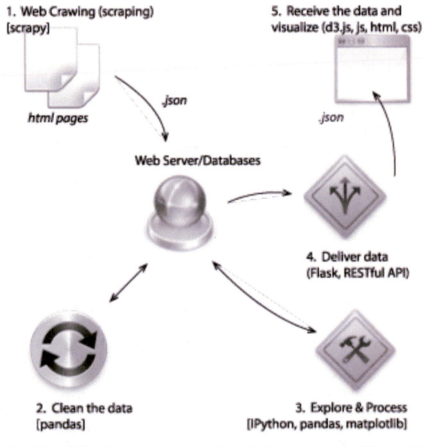

1. Web Crawling (scraping)
[scrapy]

html pages

.json

5. Receive the data and visualize (d3.js, js, html, css)

.json

Web Server/Databases

4. Deliver data (Flask, RESTful API)

2. Clean the data [pandas]

3. Explore & Process [IPython, pandas, matplotlib]

FIGURE APPENDIX B.5 Another view of an information system architecture for big data and visualization. *Courtesy of the author*

MACHINE LEARNING (ML) ACTIVITIES

The realm of ML includes many activities that are part of the preprocessing and work life of visualizations. Behind the visualizations are data that have been analyzed using a host of mathematical techniques. Some of these include Markov models, statistical language processing, artificial neural networks, Bayesian networks, classification and clustering algorithms, data mining for machine learning, dimensional reduction, and many more. To make sense of the range, ML techniques are usually divided into three groups: structured learning, unstructured learning, and semistructured learning.

Table Appendix B.1 suggests what the analysts want to achieve (prediction, classification) to create a related dataset. The challenge is to select and apply the proper algorithm.

TABLE APPENDIX B.1				
examples of unstructured data	examples of semistructured data		examples of structured data	
x400.png 9932.tif pariscalling.jpg 2018-15-05survey .png ... rk2009 .30039 .29111 BRCA1	lab-report lab-report ... gene name	x400.png 9932.tif pariscalling.jpg 2018-15-05survey .png ... rk2009 .30039 .29111 BRCA1	lab-report lab-report vacation staff-review ... license_no moles moles gene name	x400.png 9932.tif pariscalling.jpg 2018-15-05survey .png ... rk2009 .30039 .29111 BRCA1
Typical storage and sources				
analog data GSP tracking data audio/visual streams unlabeled text or data sets	.xml email .json structured text		databases data warehouses enterprise systems	

Structured learning techniques apply to data that are "labeled," that is, the data to be processed have some contextualizing metadata that helps us to cluster and classify the data before further processing. Semistructured datasets consist of data that contain a combination of labeled and unlabeled data. Unstructured data have no labels; they are just the raw data. In table Appendix B.2, the dataset consists of file names only in the unstructured example; semistructured and structured include labels (metadata) that can be integrated to classify and improve predicting the set to which the unlabeled data could likely belong.

TABLE APPENDIX B.2			
first_name	last_name	order_id	order_total
Kathleen	Cho	123456	12.34
John	Dolan	098765	98.76

Semistructured data (in a .json structure):

```
[
    {
        first_name  : "Kathleen",
        last_name   : "Cho",
        order_id    : "123456",
        order_total : "12.34"
    },
    {
        first_name  : "John",
        last_name   : "Dolan",
        order_id    : "098765",
        order_total : "98.76
    }
]
```

Structured learning consists of pairs that are studied to infer an algorithm that would generate similar results on an untested dataset. In brief, a set of data are selected (called the "training set"), cleaned, and then tested to derive an algorithm with a high probability of performing well on a much larger set. The results of performance on the larger set are compared and the algorithm adjusted accordingly. These steps are repeated until the resulting analysis is statistically reliable.

The steps progress from people identifying a concern (such as "how might we predict the chance of recidivism of youthful offenders?"), to creating a training set of data that reflects the question (such as identifying contributing factors of social life, type of prison, experience in prison, nature of the crime, education of the offender, etc.). These properties are called a "feature vector" or the set of sample data that represent the population. The mathematics of analysis impacts the final performance of the algorithm. The dataset can be too large ("curse of dimensionality") or too small and not robust enough ("overtrained" or "overfit") to handle a wider range of variance and exceptions.

First, a subset of the data are extracted and studied. This is called the training set. The algorithm used to create the candidate clustering and classification is studied for its accuracy in predicting class membership. With this actual example from a medical research lab, the researchers have collected over 30,000 questions for selecting patients for various studies. The researchers need to identify quickly and accurately a smaller set of questions, say about 15, that can be used to select the "best" questions for a given research project. In this example, the researchers' test collection of 30,000 questions reflect all aspects of diabetes. The team wants to study Type I diabetes in a certain group of juveniles. How can the team winnow out the questions that do not apply to juveniles, and then further refine the set to focus on the facets of the disease being studied?

In this situation, the researchers may randomly select 300 questions, read each one, and classify the question into one of several groups. Then the properties of those questions are identified as best as the researchers can, and are used in an algorithm to cluster and classify a vastly larger set of questions. The newly extracted set of potential questions are reviewed and measured for accuracy. Classification can be performed by human experts to determine the classification error rate. Ultimately, there are statistical tests performed on the sets to measure their similarity and accuracy. The algorithm may be revised and tested again. In short, then, we see an iterative process of selection, testing, and refining. Some of the techniques reach a stopping point on their own, such as a particular value for the mean of the group. Overall, this prefatory data clustering is termed "dimensionality reduction" or "reduction in dimensional space." Students of statistics may be familiar with some of the techniques, such as linear discriminant analysis (LDA), principal component analysis (PCA), and k-nearest neighbor algorithms, shown in figure Appendix B.6.

Semisupervised Learning

With semisupervised learning, we focus on continuity assumption or cluster assumption, meaning we start with grouping data we believe to share some important property. In the former case, data points that are close together (however mapped) are likely to share a label. For instance, say your data consists of mostly labeled data of photographs where someone has classified them into two groups: those that "contain a person in the picture" or those that "do not contain a person." An

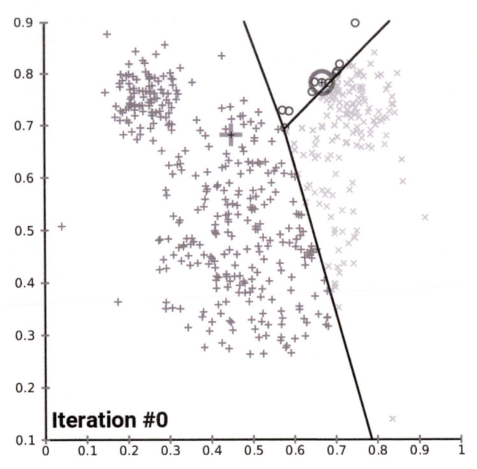

FIGURE APPENDIX B.6 A *k*-means clustering example. The printed version looks static; the web-based version dynamically updates the plot. *https://commons .wikimedia.org/wiki/File:K-means_convergence.gif*

image recognition algorithm will use this evidence as a justification for clustering the photographs with and without a person into two groups. The unlabeled data are examined for other facets that infer with high probability membership in one of the two groups. The groups are separated by a decision boundary. The boundary may be linear (latent-semantic indexing, kernel PCA, among others) or more fluid (not unlike a Kohonen feature map, force-directed, among others).

Unsupervised Learning

Unsupervised learning may be similar to data mining for hypothesis generation. Given a vast set of data, and a goal, how can we determine to a reasonable degree the most efficient path from unorganized data to an organized dataset that leads to a conclusion? There are several models to consider. For instance, if we were given a data collection of just words extracted from millions of documents, how could we begin to organize them into groups by topic ("topic modeling")? A solution might be k-means, hierarchical clustering, or any technique that expose "latent" variables—that is, relationships or facts in the data that were not otherwise evident.

Using a program that explores the dataset by testing different algorithms for clustering and then tests the data statistically generates a variety of output maps, such as a heat map or a "self-organizing map." The reasoning behind these approaches is based on biological models of how the human mind creates its own "neural maps."

Two main approaches for training here are the U-matrix and k-means. U-matrices use the similarity measure, or weight, to determine how far away from each other the data points should be visualized, often on a Euclidean grid, whereas k-means (or Lloyd's algorithm) start with a random distribution of the data points, then create a cluster of the data. Measure the least squared mean of each data point from the cluster's center. Keep updating the measurements until the data "converge," meaning the data points are not likely to move from the centroid of each cluster after another iteration.

For visualization, we can apply this readily to Voronoi diagrams (the illustration at the head of this chapter) and decision trees, among others. Students exploring Apache Hadoop may want to experiment with Mahout, a MapReduce module for k-means.

SUMMARY

In our study, the progress from subconscious to conscious association is predicated on a communicative action between the viewer, the visualization, and the viewer's own cognitive experiences. Incorporating background data (the subordinate) to the visualization (basic level), viewers passively understand the visualization. Studying the other parts of the visualization, such as advancing to the superordinate after establishing a baseline for interpretations, or adding interactivity tools and preparing the data to predict classification, advances the user experience to active learning. We need one more step to enable exploration through the graphic user interface's controls to manipulate the data as an input and cause the display to update as the output.

InfoVis practitioners participate in making any data more useful, be they library use statistics, exposing relationships between words and concepts from literature, or exposing causes and effects from large datasets. The size and variability of the data in these large datasets require us to apply strong computational techniques and an understanding of data types.

The study of information visualization has become "scientized," or systematized, echoing the rule-based concept learning that Bruner and his colleagues (2009) proposed. Trying to organize every visual element in graphs reached a high point with Bertin's 1967 *Sémiologie* and, later Ward, Grinstein, and Keim's (2015) exhaustive catalogue of imagery. In a computing setting this is not unreasonable, given the mathematical orientation of computer scientists and the computer technology, essentially a high-energy grid paper, that has guided notions of the arts and of data since the 1950s (Lunenfeld, 2001).

I believe by learning more about data, how people interact with art, theories of cognition and communication, and applying the whole to a domain—here information science—we understand more about what it means to learn, how we learn, and provide a real justification for our efforts in popularizing InfoVis in any information profession. Students of information visualization today need at least a passing knowledge of the link between the bigger picture of coding, computer networks, and visualization.

HANDS-ON PRACTICE

For this exercise, we look at trees as part of machine learning. Refer to Table Appendix B.3.

TABLE APPENDIX B.3			
Data Point	**Value**	**Data Point**	**Value**
1	A	11	
2	A	12	
3	A	13	B
4		14	A
5	B	15	C
6	A	16	A
7	A	17	A
8	B	18	B
9	B	19	B
10	B	20	

1. Given this set of data points, how would you determine where the unlabeled data points are to be classified? (You'll have to create a scenario for the data, create a goal, and establish what rules you'd apply to classify some of the data).

2. Given this same set, create a decision tree. (For this you will need to establish rules that would determine where to put each data point; create a scenario, decide the cutoff values, create example charts.)
3. Using your decision tree from question 2, draw a tree map. Identify the number of regions. What about values that are shared between regions?

REFERENCES

Bertin, J. (1967). *Sémiologie graphique: les diagrammes, les réseaux, les cartes.* Paris: Gauthier-Villars.

Bruner, J. S., Goodnow, J. J., & Austin, G. A. (2009). *A study of thinking.* New Brunswick: Transaction. Originally published 1956.

Chater, N., Lyon, K., & Myers, T. (1990). Why are conjunctive categories overextended? *Journal of Experimental Psychology: Leaning, Memory, and Cognition, 16*(3), 497–508.

Klausmeier, H. J. (1980). *Learning and teaching concepts.* New York, NY: Academic Press.

Lunenfeld, P. (2001). *Snap to grid: A user's guide to digital arts, media, and cultures.* Cambridge, MA: MIT Press.

Posner, M. I. & Keele, S. W. (1968). On the genesis of abstract ideas. *Journal of Experimental Psychology, 77*, 353–63.

Rosch, E., Mervis, C. B., Gray, W., Johnson, D., & Boyes-Braem, P. (1976). Basic objects in natural categories. *Cognitive Psychology, 8*, 382–440.

Tennyson, R. D., & Cocchiarella, M. J. (1986). An empirically-based instructional design theory for teaching concepts. *Review of Educational Research, 56*(1), 40–71.

University of Indiana. (2017). Concept learning. Retrieved September 28, 2018, from http://cognitrn.psych.indiana.edu/rgoldsto/courses/concepts2.pdf

Ward, M., Grinstein, G., & Keim, D. (2015). *Interactive data visualization.* New York, NY: CRC.

INDEX

ABOUT THE AUTHOR

Gerald Benoît earned his doctorate from the University of California, Los Angeles (UCLA), writing on Habermas's *The Theory of Communicative Action*, and applied this complex critical theory to human-human and human-computer communication. Before pursuing an academic career, teaching programming, information architecture, systems analysis, theory, statistics, and visual communication, Benoît was a programmer/analyst for the University of California, an information specialist for Price Waterhouse, and the art director/partner in the marketing firm Imada, Wong, Park, & Benoît.

As a consultant, Professor Benoît remains active helping large and smaller organizations understand their data resources, integrate information systems, and create new information services and systems, such as interactive information visualization apps for the Harvard Libraries, Boston Public Library, Peabody-Essex Museum, and biomedical and other firms.

Benoît has long been interested in arts, languages, and technology. He earned a master's degree from Columbia University, where he focused on rare materials, and from the University of California, Davis, double-majoring in French and Russian. Benoît translates materials from Russian, Spanish, French, and German for articles and monographs. He also serves as an officer in ASIST SIG-VIS, as a faculty member at Harvard College's Adams House Senior Common Room, and regularly reviews for IEEE, SIG-IR, communications theory, and philosophy.

Today Benoît teaches for the University of California, Berkeley's data science program and builds enterprise-wide, web-enabled database applications and responsive interfaces. Read more about Professor Benoit, his CV, and publications at https://bix.digital/index.html.